CROCKER'S FOLLY

The Development of, and Opposition to, the Palm Springs Aerial Tramway

Steve Lech

Published by the author

Table of Contents

Introduction

Postcard view of Mt. San Jacinto by Stephen Willard, c. 1935 (Author's collection).

Anyone who has heard about the Palms Springs Aerial Tramway, and certainly has ridden it, has heard the oft-told story of how it began. One hot day in what is generally given as 1935, Francis Crocker of Palm Springs looked up at Mt. San Jacinto and thought there could and should be an easy way to get up to it and enjoy the cooler temperatures. Nearly 30 years later and after hundreds of helicopter flights to construct it over a two-year period, the tramway opened.

For me, a local historian who has been interested in Riverside County's history for over 40 years, this explanation wasn't enough. Why did it take so long? When one attempts to delve a little bit into why, one is told that material shortages during two wars were to blame for the tramway's long hiatus. To me, though, that still wasn't enough. Therefore, I started hunting in earnest.

What I soon discovered is that there was a widespread effort, both locally and at the State and National levels, to thwart the construction of the tramway – and that this seems never to be discussed in any of the popular accounts of the tram. Many people put forth good, well-thought-out arguments against construction of the tram, and with good reason – the facility we know now, namely the tram and its two stations – was only the tip of the iceberg when it came to development both in the desert and atop the mountain. Originally envisioned as a gateway to a winter sports complex in Long Valley, the Palm Springs Aerial Tramway was to lead to ski slopes, restaurants, hotels, toboggan runs, and a whole host of other uses. It was not simply the up-and-down the mountain thrill ride it is today.

Another aspect of this fight soon occurred to me from the standpoint of someone who was involved in planning issues in Riverside County. In essence, the effort to keep the Palm Springs Aerial Tramway from being built was the first large-scale environmental battle to be waged in Riverside County. Today, these types of conflicts happen regularly when a development proposal is brought forth and is contested due to sensitivity of biological or cultural resources. In post-war Riverside County, though, nothing like that had occurred before. Sure, there were environmental concerns about preserving open space and natural areas, but they were largely agreed upon by everyone, and areas were set aside as a proactive means of preserving lands BEFORE there were development proposals. As the reader will see in the ensuing pages, reacting to a development proposal by lobbying for preservation was a new way of seeing things at this time, and the ensuing confusion and discord goes a long way to showing that no one had actually thought about this scenario beforehand in Riverside County.

This book is not meant to be an exhaustive history of the Tram. Obviously, I can't detail one side of the story without relating the other, but the emphasis here is in the opposition - the story that, outside of a dissertation that is all but overlooked now, has never really been told.

Also, this book will not detail the construction of the tram - that is done very ably by James Landells in his book *We Can Do It: The Construction of the Palm Springs Aerial Tramway*. Landells' father was Don Landells, one of the helicopter pilots who flew many missions to deliver men and materiale to the sites. The reader is encouraged to read this book in conjunction with that one.

It is my hope that you the reader will enjoy learning the back story of one of Riverside County's most iconic tourist attractions. It was a hard-fought battle, pitting well-connected business interests in Palm Springs against those who had very sound arguments against commercializing the conserved areas of the San Jacinto Mountains. As we know now, what ensued was in essence a compromise, one that continues to attract people by the thousands.

Acknowledgments

Obviously, a project such as this cannot be undertaken alone. Luckily, I was fortunate to have met many people who helped me greatly in any way they could. These include;

Renee Brown *(Director of Education/Associate Curator, Palm Springs Historical Society)*

Tracy Conrad *(President, Palm Springs Historical Society)*

Dr. Jennifer Gee *(Director, James San Jacinto Mountains Reserve)*

Jessica Geiser *(Collections Management Librarian, Special Collections & University Archives, UCR Library)*

Kitty Kieley *(Palm Springs historian and granddaughter of O. Earl Coffman)*

James Landells *(Author of* We Can Do It: The Construction of the Palm Springs Aerial Tramway *and a great source for photos)*

Todd B. McMeans, PE *(Senior Vice President, Modjeski and Masters, Inc).*

Madison Morgan *(Public Relations Manager, Palm Springs Aerial Tramway)*

Karen Raines *(Special Collections Public Services Coordinator, UCR Special Collections & University Archives)*

Kristina Vasquez *(Records Management Program, California State Parks Department)*

Nancy Wenzel *(for proofreading!)*

Ian M. Wright *(Assistant Director, James San Jacinto Mountains Reserve)*

Morgan Yates *(Corporate Archivist, Automobile Club of Southern California)*

Lena Zimmerschied *(Former Public Affairs Manager, Palm Springs Aerial Tramway)*

Last week a young man, wearing dungarees and boots and carrying a water canteen and knapsack, met another your man dressed in sport shirt, slacks and wearing loafers.

The meeting place was on an elaborate platform overlooking Palm Springs and the Coachella Valley desert floor more than 8500 feet below.

It had taken one of the youths six hours to climb Mt. San Jacinto into the "high country." The other reached the same point in 15 minutes.

One had started his nine mile hike up the rugged slope of Mt. San Jacinto from Idyllwild, California, on the west side of the range. The other made his ascent from the valley station of the just opened Palm Springs Aerial Tramway, an amazing engineering project which started as a "wild dream" 25 years ago.

Jack Pepper, "Two Ways to the Tramway,"
Desert Magazine, October, 1963

Postcard view of Chino Canyon, 1940s (Author's collection).

Chapter 1

Beginnings

> *What is being done to make (our mountain) more accessible to our winter visitors? Has anyone made any serious attempt to actually bring about the construction of the tramway from Palm Springs to Round Valley? . . . . Such a railway would be one of the best investments the state could make to increase the tourist crop, which, after all, is the state's most profitable crop."*
>
> *Carl Barkow, editorial in* The Desert Sun, *October 22, 1937.*

Exactly when the concept for an aerial tramway to whisk passengers from the desert floor to San Jacinto Mountain came about is uncertain. Most sources agree it was 1935, and some even get specific enough to say it was July of that year. What is certain is that two men, Francis Crocker, a 35-year-old electrical engineer with the Nevada-California Electric Corporation stationed in Palm Springs, and Carl Barkow, the then-editor of *The Desert Sun* newspaper, were in Palm Springs on a hot day and admiring the towering San Jacinto Mountains abutting the city to the west. Crocker believed that it would be nice to be able to quickly get to the cooler temperatures at the higher altitudes. Barkow told him that only a few years before, the Southern Pacific Railroad, which owned a huge amount of land within the San Jacinto Mountains and Coachella Valley, had contemplated putting some form of a lift from the San Gorgonio Pass up the steep face of Mt. San Jacinto for just the same purpose Crocker was envisioning.

Escaping the heat of either the desert of the Coachella Valley or the semi desert of most of Southern California by traveling to the San Jacinto Mountains had been the practice of people for thousands of years. Local Indians migrated between the desert and mountains on a seasonal basis following game, plant materials, and the warmer or cooler temperatures. Beginning in the 1870s, Americans who were settling in Southern California began establishing commercial camps in the mountains to which people could escape and relax during the summer heat. At this time, access to the San Jacinto Mountains was, for the most part, limited to well-worn trails and would require a trek of a few days to find respite.

Early view of the Hemet-Idyllwild road (Author's collection).

That began to change in 1870 when Joseph Crawford established a toll road between Hemet and Strawberry Valley where the present town of Idyllwild is located. This road was treacherous and not well maintained. In an effort to improve access, the road was declared abandoned by the San Diego County Board of Supervisors (as Riverside County had not yet been established), and became a public road. Several modifications and route changes later, this route became the Hemet-Idyllwild Road. Beginning in 1926, Riverside County undertook to upgrade the road and it was officially opened three years later as a new, high-gear road to the mountains.

Similarly, in 1902, people in the towns of Banning and Beaumont asked for access to the mountains. Surveys were completed, and a new road was begun in 1905. This road went as far as the present-day Lake Fulmor area – not all the way to Idyllwild, but certainly into the higher elevations. Under a new contract, work was initiated in 1909 and the Banning-Idyllwild road was completed in 1910.

In the late 1910s and early 1920s, residents of the Coachella Valley asked for a road to go from the desert to the mountains. Originally, the road was to start in Palm Springs and head south through Palm Canyon to Vandeventer Flats, then northwest through Garner Valley to Idyllwild. Lobbyists from Indio, including newspaper publisher J. Win Wilson and farmer Wilson Howell, pushed incessantly for the road to come closer to their town and bypass Palm Springs. Several

Later view of the Hemet-Idyllwild Road (Author's collection).

Pines-to-Palms Highway, 1932 (Author's collection).

Later view of the Banning-Idyllwild Road (Author's collection).

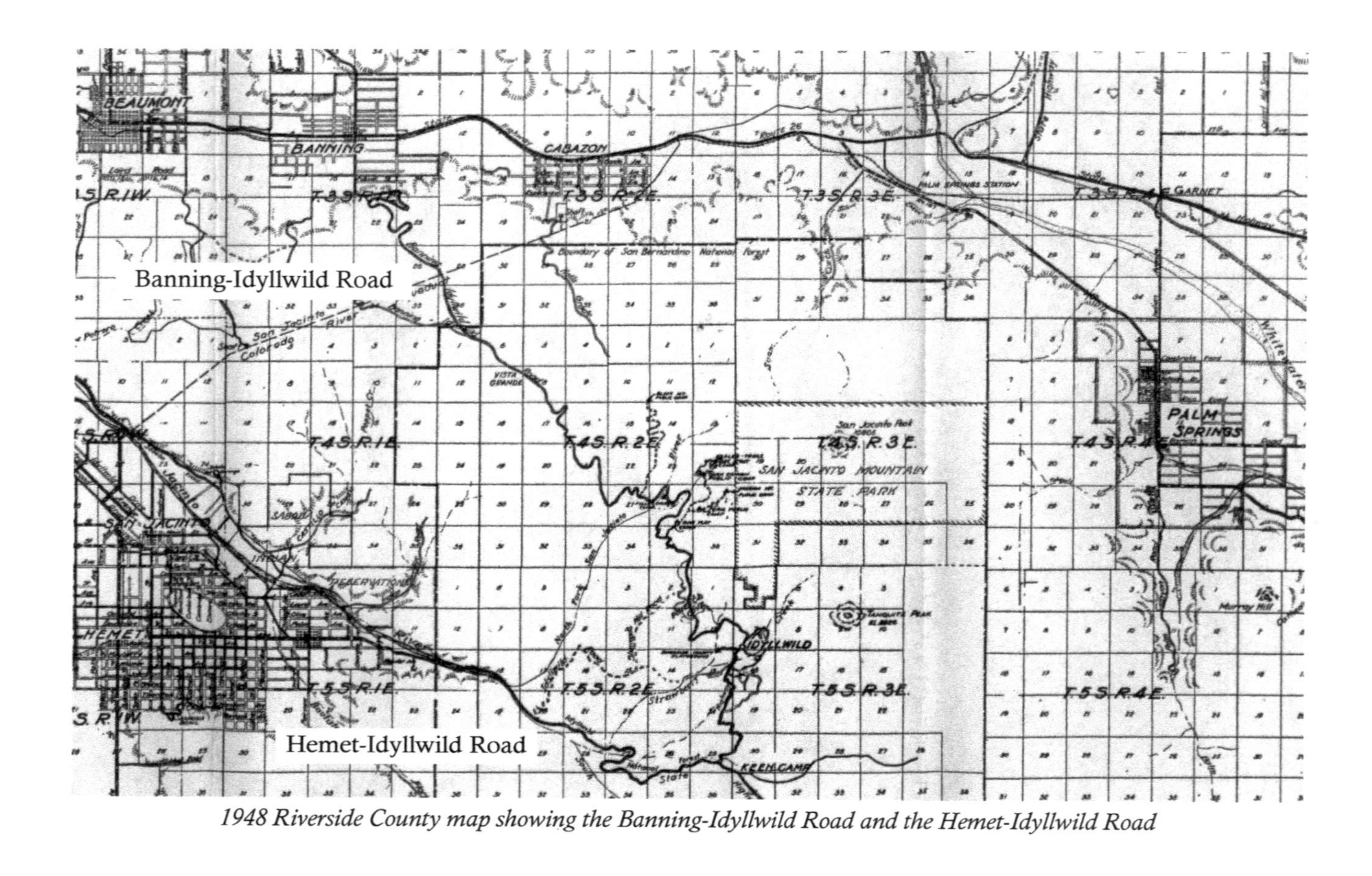

1948 Riverside County map showing the Banning-Idyllwild Road and the Hemet-Idyllwild Road

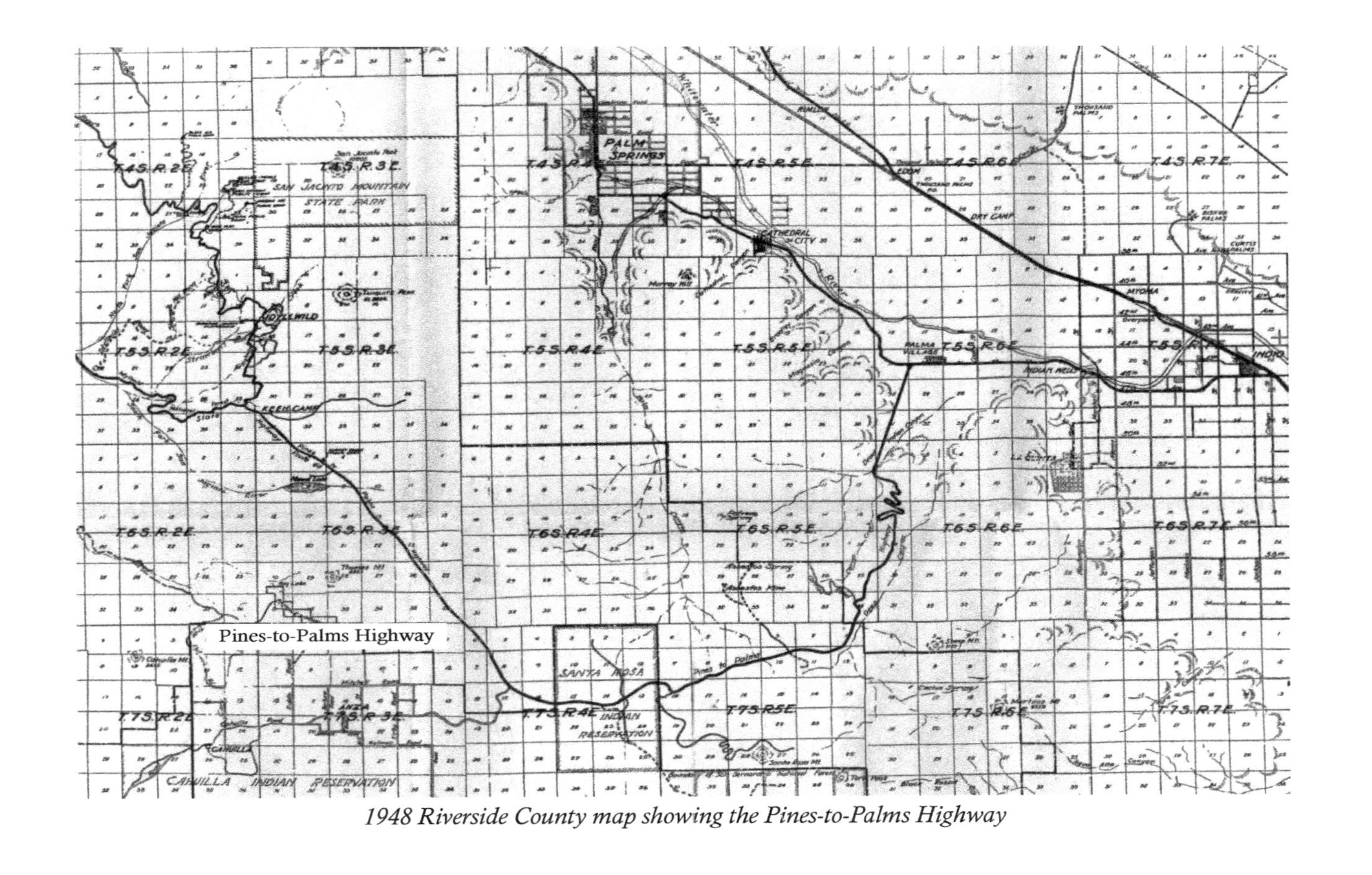

1948 Riverside County map showing the Pines-to-Palms Highway

factors worked in their favor, and the end result was the creation of the Pines-to-Palms Highway, which connected the San Jacinto Mountains with the Palm Springs-Indio Highway near Indio, at the present-day location of the City of Palm Desert.[1]

In addition to the roads, there had already been talk of scaling the San Jacinto Mountains by other means. As far back as 1909 there was a whimsical mention of an alternative method of reaching the high San Jacintos when the Banning *Record* reported that Harold A. E. Marshall, the Supervisor of the Cleveland National Forest, had discovered a lake near San Jacinto Peak. The *Record* editorialized that, "this spot would make a delightful summer resort, but a person in order to reach it ought to have an incline railway . . ."[2]

The idea of some form of incline railway began to take hold in the early 1920s. The Southern Pacific Railroad, eager to get passengers from its line through the San Gorgonio Pass up to the cooler climes, began to seriously consider the prospects of some form of "elevator" either to San Jacinto Peak via Snow Creek Canyon or to Tahquitz Peak via Tahquitz Canyon. By 1926, enough consideration had been given that a party of engineers and officers from the railroad went on a scouting tour of both peaks to consider the proposal. Realizing that the Swiss used funiculars to scale Alpine peaks, the Southern Pacific engineers gave at least some consideration to making such a system a

Snow Creek escarpment of Mt. San Jacinto (Author's photo).

reality in the San Jacinto Mountains. They also considered creating a better trail system between the peaks, and an automobile road to connect them with Idyllwild for vacationers. There seems to have been little else accomplished toward this goal beyond the initial surveys.[3]

Therefore, by 1935, when Crocker and Barkow were looking longingly at the higher regions of the San Jacinto Mountains, there had already been three roads, countless trails, and at least one semi-serious attempt at a cable-car "elevator" system that could take people to or from the mountains. To Crocker and Barkow's dismay, though, none of these major routes of travel went through or to Palm Springs. In an era when tourist dollars were a major portion of the economic base of many towns, including Palm Springs, this situation was unacceptable.[4]

Over the next two years, Crocker continued working at the Nevada-California Electric Corporation, and in his spare time kept his thought for an aerial conveyance system to the top of the mountain in his mind. While earlier attempts generally centered around a system to go up Snow Creek to San Jacinto Peak, Crocker thought that it might be more practical to use either Chino Canyon or Tahquitz Canyon. Tahquitz Canyon would be almost impossible to use, though, given that the Agua Caliente Indians owned the property and were steadfast in their refusal to sell or lease any part of it.[5] Luckily, Chino Canyon, in Crocker's eyes, seemed the most appropriate.

By June, 1937, Crocker had talked up his proposal enough, and done an adequate amount of preliminary work, to approach the local Lions club about the scheme. On June 10, Crocker met with the group and outlined his plan for a "funicular railway to San Jacinto peak." Here, he proposed to connect Chino Canyon at 3,500 feet in elevation with Round Valley at 8,500 feet.[6] In establishing his proposal, though, Crocker had to come up with some hook to tie the railway into the tourist trade in Palm Springs. Instead of simply building an elevator to nowhere, it would be touted for its appeal to winter sports enthusiasts. Francis Crocker's proposal met with accolades from the group.

Crocker had already been working with associates in Los Angeles. Two days before his presentation to the Palm Springs Lions Club, the proposed tramway was mentioned by Ed Ainsworth in the Los Angeles *Times*. Ainsworth's column, entitled "Along El Camino Real," mentioned Crocker's efforts, and due to Ainsworth's popularity, the project began to be talked about throughout the Los Angeles basin in addition to the Coachella Valley.[7]

The Lions Club was so enthusiastic that Crocker came back the next week to further discuss issues related to the tramway. He indicated that the Southern Pacific Railroad would not be interested in financing such a project, as they were not in the resort business. However, there could be several entities in Los Angeles who might, and he was heading to that city to begin the promotion of the project.[8] Crocker's vision for the venture was not without its detractors at this time. Jimmy Cooper, writing for a vacationing Carl Barkow in *The Desert Sun*, editorialized that,

> Francis Crocker, local manager of the Nevada-California Electric Corporation, recreator of the idea of constructing a tramway from Chino Canyon up to Round Valley . . . said friends and associates were 'kidding' him about the idea, calling it 'Crocker's Folly' and such names. . . . The writer is just as enthusiastic as Mr. Crocker is about such a tramway.[9]

One of the ways Crocker sold his proposed funicular railway was by indicating that "Round Valley . . . is as suitable for winter sports as famous Sun Valley in Idaho, which is being exploited by the Union Pacific Railroad. . . There is an abundance of snow in Round Valley from early winter until late in the spring, and is ideally situated for skiing and tobogganing."[10] These statements introduced a new audience that was on the minds of many in Southern California at the time – winter sports enthusiasts.

Skiers in Idyllwild, c. 1930s (Author's collection).

Ever since the 1932 Winter Olympic games in Lake Placid, New York, there had been a surge in interest in skiing in the United States, and particularly the west, where many mountains and mountain ranges, hitherto known only for their remoteness and wilderness qualities, were being considered for their potential for winter sports development. In Southern California, the San Gabriel Mountains and the San Bernardino Mountains were touted for their potential, and even the San Jacinto Mountains were too, albeit to a lesser extent. However, in the minds of potential developers, every place had its potential, and there were many people who stood ready to champion any place in which they may have an interest.

"Skiing is here to stay . . ." wrote Ethel Severson in 1937 to the Mountain League of Southern California. "Skiing is the perfect sport . . . Its appeal is universal . . . watch it – and you'll see the enlivening spectacle of California taking to skiing!"[11] At the same time, the Riverside *Press* reported that Frank Robinson, the supervisor of the San Bernardino National Forest, which includes the San Jacinto Mountains, was on record stating that the San Jacinto Mountain area was ripe for winter sports development:

> There are three regions suggested as logical locations for such a resort [as Sun Valley Idaho]. They are the west side of the San Jacinto Mountains and the north side of San Gorgonio and Keller peaks.
>
> These areas he said are particularly well adapted for skiing, with wide expanses of uniform slopes for the novice and more precipitous inclines for the experts. Because of their high elevations, snow is abundant throughout the winter and up to April.
>
> By implication, of the three locations the San Jacinto area apparently offers the most favorable conditions for development for snow sports. It is pointed out that the San Gorgonio slope is in a primitive area, and as such, the erection of any type of permanent fixture is forbidden. . . .
>
> . . . Doubtless the San Jacinto Mountain Chamber of Commerce . . . will seize on this opportunity as one which may well enlist the interest and support of all portions of Riverside County. Southern Californians, not excluding a lot of Riversiders, are only just coming to realize the importance

of the San Jacinto mountain area as a natural asset, and its possibilities for further development as a winter and summer playground.[12]

A year later, noted rock climber and ski enthusiast Glen Dawson reported that Helen Henderson of Palm Springs was planning a series of ski trips into the San Jacinto Mountains from that city.[13] By 1939, the Palm Springs *Limelight* newspaper was really at the forefront of trying to encourage winter sports development in the San Jacinto Mountains:

> There are several outstanding advantages to be gained through the construction of the Aerial Tramway project. Primarily it would open up a tremendous winter sports area for skiing, tobogganing and ice skating within fifteen minutes of the already developed resort of Palm Springs and its large pleasure-seeking tourist population.
>
> At present this great sports asset is an untouched resource. If it is to keep its lead as a winter sports and vacation land, Southern California must open up new fields to meet the competition offered by such places as Sun Valley. This new winter resort does pretty well with no other asset than perfect skiing country and fine hotels.
>
> During the past winter an experienced ski enthusiast made a careful survey of Round Valley, the highest station of the San Jacinto Aerial Tramway. He was thoroughly familiar with the best skiing territories both in this country and abroad. He found in Round Valley what he rated a perfect ski country – long, gradual slopes for the novice, free of trees, "naturals" he called them, and mile long steep inclines to challenge the expert ski-man. Also in this area is Hidden Lake which could be developed into an ice skaters' paradise.[14]

One of the criticisms endured at the time by Crocker's proposal was that nothing like it had been attempted in the United States. European countries such as Switzerland and Austria had had various cable transport systems for several years, but none existed in the U. S. It soon came to light, though, that in fact another such project was being proposed in the United States, and it was actually well on its way toward completion when Crocker was making his initial announcements.

In the late 1920s and early 1930s, Cannon Mountain in north-central New Hampshire was a favorite ski location for Alexander Bright, a famous skier from the region. On a trip to Europe in 1933, he saw how cable lifts were used to take skiers up mountains, and he wanted to do the same back in New Hampshire. He persuaded several influential people to conduct surveys of the Franconia Notch section of Mt. Cannon State Park.[15] Included in those influential people were a wealthy family by the name of Peckett who were developing their Sugar Hill Inn into a winter destination resort complete with ski school and slope.[16] By 1937, when Francis Crocker was invigorating local support for a cableway up Mt. San Jacinto, the State Legislature of New Hampshire approved a $250,000 bond for the construction of the Cannon Mountain Aerial Tramway.[17] On June 21, 1938, Cannon Mountain's aerial tramway opened, and over the next several years, this tramway would be the pattern for much of Crocker's work towards constructing a similar project on Mt. San Jacinto.[18]

Cannon Mountain Aerial Tramway, c. 1938 (Author's collection).

As can be seen, due to many reasons, Francis Crocker's idea of a tramway to Mt. San Jacinto was quickly gaining ground in the region. Not only did the idea have what turned out to be a consummate pitchman in the form of Crocker, but the idea of winter sports was beginning to gain ground in Southern California's mountain regions, and 3,000 miles away, it was being shown that a cable tramway could in fact be a reality in the United States. Therefore, throughout the late 1930s, several important business and civic leaders joined with Crocker to become a forceful, unified voice for developing the Mt. San Jacinto Aerial Tramway and putting Palm Springs on the map as a winter sports mecca. Some of these people included Alvah Hicks, the manager of the Palm Springs Water Company and a 20+ year resident of the town, Carl Lykken, owner of the town's first self-proclaimed "department store," Philip Boyd, who at the time was a real estate investor and banker but who would later become Palm Springs' first mayor (after 1938) and later, a State Senator from the region, Culver Nichols, a former Hollywood realtor who was now living in the desert, Warren Pinney, the influential manager of the El Mirador Hotel, John Chaffey, a long-time area realtor, and Owen Earl Coffman, son of Palm Springs pioneer Nellie Coffman and owner of the famed Desert Inn.[19] Most of these men were appointed by the Palm Springs Chamber of Commerce to assist in any way to bring about the tramway. Over the next several years, they would work tirelessly to see that the project came to fruition.

For Crocker and the group to talk up the prospect of a desert-to-mountain cable system was one thing, but the practicality of such a proposal, both from an engineering and financial standpoint, was entirely another. Crocker, an electrical engineer by training, could only do so much. Therefore, by late 1937, he and the others began to enlist the aid of outside engineers, in addition to just about anyone who would listen. In January, 1938, it was announced that Joseph Strauss, an engineer with more than 500 bridges to his credit, not the least of which was the recently-completed Golden Gate Bridge, remarked that the proposal was "not only feasible, but would undoubtedly net a handsome profit to the group financing the plan."[20]

Going hand-in-hand with Strauss' assessment came a report from two rugged Palm Springs hikers who undertook to hike the route of the proposed tramway. Starting in Long Valley after a hike to that location from Idyllwild, Phil Kaspar and Jim Maynard hiked down to the foot of Chino Canyon and reported their findings to various groups and *The Desert Sun* (their account of the hike is reproduced as Appendix A).

By the spring of 1939, Crocker was ready to pitch the project to the Palm Springs Planning Commission. Crocker hoped to keep the venture local, and was trying to get support from the city. He had also secured the intense interest of Frank Masters, an engineer of wide fame and part namesake of the firm of Modjeski and Masters in Harrisburg, Pennsylvania. Masters was so interested in the potential of the project that he promised that his firm would undertake to conduct an engineering feasibility report and cost estimate for the project for around $2,000 if there was enough local support for it. Crocker made his usual pitch about how the proposal would benefit Palm Springs and open it up as a winter sports resort, but noted that it should not be "a private, highly promotional venture, as it would, because of its spectacular attraction, require some civic control."[21]

The Planning Commission opted to study the plan in more detail and did not take action, but many of the members supported the idea. Most of them supported it for the reasons generally given (tourism, winter sports), but one, City Planner William Reis, expressed trepidation. Stating that the proposed figure of some 600 tourists a day could ride the tram, Reis worried about all of those people congesting the streets of the city. He also envisioned busloads of people coming with the sole purpose of marveling at the engineering wonder that would be the tramway, but not riding it. The *Limelight* summed up people's feelings about Reis' concerns thusly – "He was a minority of one."[22]

By the spring of 1939, the Planning Commission was on board with Crocker's proposal, and representatives from other engineering firms and steel manufacturing firms also lent their support for the unique undertaking. All of the planning, figuring, and engineering that had been done so far by optimistic Crocker and others had led to the belief that the construction of a cable tramway up to Mt. San Jacinto could be done. However, before the proposal could enter the next phase, a true engineering feasibility report would have to be done, and with it an actual estimate by a professional estimator so that the promoters could have a solid foundation of facts and statistics from which to work. Modjeski and Masters would have to get to work.

Chapter 1 Endnotes

1. For the full history of the efforts to construct the Pines-to-Palms Highway, see my 2012 book, *For Tourism and a Good Night's Sleep – J. Win Wilson, Wilson Howell, and the Beginnings of the Pines-to-Palms Highway.*
2. Banning *Record*, August 5, 1909.
3. Hemet *News*, July 2, 1926.
4. The reader should bear in mind that from about the 1870s through the 1940s, the tourism industry in Southern California was a major economic powerhouse. In addition, tourists were potential investors in a community, and not just someone coming through to visit a site and move on. Towns, cities, and communities actively competed with one another for tourists, and any tourist amenity, such as a new major hotel, resort, mode of transportation, or scenic vista was touted as another bit of success in the ever-present desire to lure more and more tourists to various towns. Having roads leading into the San Jacinto Mountains from Hemet, Banning, and the open area between Palm Springs and Indio did little to help Palm Springs' efforts at increasing tourism to that town.
5. Attempts in the 1910s and 1920s to create a national park and/or national monument out of Tahquitz Canyon had fallen on deaf ears so far as the Agua Caliente were concerned. Likewise, the tribe had shut off free access to Palm Canyon in 1931 during the campaign to get the Pines-to-Palms Highway aligned down that canyon instead of through Carrizo and Dead Indian Canyon to the southeast.
6. *The Desert Sun*, June 11, 1937.
7. Ainsworth, Ed. "Along El Camino Real." Los Angeles *Times*, June 8, 1937.
8. *The Desert Sun*, June 18, 1937.
9. *Ibid.*
10. *Ibid.*
11. "Skiing Has Come to Stay." Trails Magazine (The Mountain League of Southern California), Vol. 4, No. 4, pp 8-11, 19: Autumn 1937.
12. Riverside *Press*, September 11, 1937.
13. "Ski Touring and Ski Mountaineering." Trails Magazine (The Mountain League of Southern California), Vol. 5, No. 4, pp 8-10: Autumn 1938.
14. Palm Springs *Limelight*, January 14, 1939.
15. See Chapter 4 for a discussion of the implications of the tramway running through a state park.

16. New England Ski History, Cannon Mountain, Franconia New Hampshire. http://www.newenglandskihistory.com/NewHampshire/cannonmtn.php, accessed March 26, 2016.
17. "Cannon History." http://cannonmt.com/cannon-history.html, accessed April 2, 2016.
18. *Ibid.*
19. Davis, August 1973, p. 137.
20. *The Desert Sun*, January 28, 1938.
21. Palm Springs *Limelight*, April 1, 1939.
22. *Ibid.*

Chapter 2

The Modjeski and Masters Report

A study of the profiles developed eliminates any type of installation other than an aerial cableway. The mountain sides are too rugged for the construction of any type of fixed track with haulage actuated with cables or gears of the construction of a monorail type similarly powered.

Report on the Proposed Passenger Tramway up Mt. San Jacinto at Palm Springs, California, April, 1940, p. 7.

Throughout 1939 and 1940, Francis Crocker and the group of interested individuals had kept in close contact with R. G. Cone and Frank Masters of Modjeski and Masters. Now that it was time to "put their money where their mouth was" and commence a serious investigation of the project, they turned to Modjeski and Masters to give them the hard information they needed. In order to complete this study, the firm indicated that their fee would be slightly higher, at approximately $2,500. Now the backers had to come up with the money. On January 2, 1940, a large meeting of most of the members involved in the planning of the aerial tramway was held at the El Mirador Hotel in Palm

El Mirador Hotel, Palm Springs, 1941 (Author's collection).

Springs. At this meeting, $2,000 was pledged toward the completion of the report. Francis Crocker agreed to sign the contract with Modjeski and Masters when the additional $500 was raised. Estimates of 60 days to complete the report meant that the group would probably have a great deal more information to work with by the spring of 1940.[1] Within a month, Crocker had an additional $900 in his possession, and work on the survey commenced on January 26.[2]

The report was to answer a series of questions regarding the construction and operation of a proposed tramway:

1. Would the construction of an aerial tramway such as the one proposed be practical?
   a. If not, would another form of lift be more practical?
2. If construction of the project were practical, would it be feasible?
3. What would be the best route for the project to take – via Tahquitz Canyon, Chino Canyon, or Snow Creek Canyon to San Jacinto Peak?
4. What would be the estimated cost of construction of the recommended type of transportation?
5. What would be the estimated amount of traffic[3] to be generated by such a proposal?
6. What would be the estimated costs of operation of the proposal, and what would be the net earnings of such a proposal?
7. What recommended methods of financing the proposed project would be available and practical?

Throughout February and March, 1940, Modjeski and Masters performed several studies relative to the proposed tramway, with the point of it being to "study and recommend a satisfactory means of providing suitable transportation from Palm Springs to the top of Mt. San Jacinto."[4] By April, they had made their determinations, and while they were generally favorable to the project, there were some hurdles that would have to be overcome. To begin with, the report cited many favorable conditions in Palm Springs to warrant such a project:

> Palm Springs . . . is a desert oasis of unique charm, ideal for winter vacations. It is protected from the west winds and

REPORT

on the

PROPOSED PASSENGER TRAMWAY

up

MT. SAN JACINTO

at

PALM SPRINGS, CAL.

Submitted to the

PALM SPRINGS TRAMWAY FUND COMMITTEE

by

MODJESKI and MASTERS
Consulting Engineers

and

R. G. CONE
Associate Engineer

April, 1940

Cover of the Modjeski and Masters report, April, 1940 (Modjeski and Masters archives).

winter storms by the lofty San Jacinto mountains, at whose base the City lies. The San Jacinto mountains are among the most precipitous in America and rise to a height of 10,000 feet above the City of Palm Springs, so that within the distance of five miles from the City, there exists a wilderness area at an altitude of from 8,000 to 10,000 feet that is covered with a deep fall of snow on the northern slopes throughout the winter. The unusual climatic conditions have established for the City of Palm Springs a reputation as one of the foremost winter playgrounds. Because of these features, the City has shown a remarkable growth. Weather reports show an average of 350 days of clear weather annually. The tourist season begins in October and lasts until about the first of June. During the winter the days are warm and sunny and the nights of unusual clearness. The desert climate attracts many persons and consideration has been given for some time past to a proposal for the construction of a means of transportation from the valley floor to the upper wilderness areas of Mount San Jacinto in order to make available an area for winter sports, which have been greatly stimulated in recent years due to the growing enthusiasm for sports, such as skiing, tobogganing and skating.[5]

Palm Springs, 1947 (Author's collection).

road up Chino Canyon, upper and lower terminal buildings, parking lots, publicity costs, contingency costs, first-year's interest costs, and other items were factored into the estimation, the actual estimated cost ballooned to $1,360,000 (or approximately $28,500,000 in 2023 dollars).[11] Additionally, the report estimated that it would require approximately $130,000 per year to operate the tramway, and that revenues generated would be approximately $300,000. Although it was believed that revenues would outpace operation costs, paying off the initial $1,360,000 construction cost would take quite a long time given the anticipated revenues.[12]

Traffic generated by such a project had been a major concern for the proponents – would there be too many people, thus playing into the hands of William Reis of the Palm Springs Planning Commission when he stated that the roads in town could become clogged with tourists? It did not seem so. On the other hand, the traffic numbers shown in the study could be used as a method of promoting the project, enticing business owners to realize the potential influx of customers they may have due to the project. Interestingly, unlike traffic studies today, these engineers were counting how many people could potentially come to the tramway, and not how many automobile trips would be generated by the project. Regardless, the report estimated that people would come from four different areas: 1) Highway traffic passing through Palm Springs, 2) East-west traffic along Highway 60-70-99 through Whitewater (essentially today's I-10 freeway), 3) Additional patrons who might come from the area within a radius of 120 miles . . . who in one year would be expected to take one ride on the tramway if properly advertised, and 4) Winter sports enthusiasts from the same area as 3. All of this was based on the engineers' estimates of tramway operation only during the "tourist season" of the year - December 1 to April 30. Because Palm Springs had yet to become a year-round resort and there were few if any hotels that remained open during the summer months, the engineers figured that it would not be worthwhile to operate the tramway from May through November. Given all of these factors, it was anticipated that the tramway could attract approximately 150,000 people during the 4-month season. Using a fee of $2 per person to ride the tram, the report indicated that yearly revenue would be around $300,000.[13]

Finally, the report addressed how such a project could be financed. The report noted that since much of the route of the proposed tramway would be in some form of public ownership,[14] having the tramway owned and operated by a private corporation would be highly objectionable. Likewise, one of the biggest parties involved in such a project, namely the City of Palm Springs, would not have a say in the operation of the tramway if a private corporation were brought in to build and operate it. Therefore, the report recommended that a public authority authorized to issue bonds be created to handle the project. These types of authorities had been used successfully throughout the country to finance and construct such infrastructure as toll roads and toll bridges, and the engineers recommended that the tramway project be treated similarly, if in fact such a method was allowed in the State of California. Another benefit of the public authority method would be the acquisition of rights-of-way. Since portions of the proposed tramway would lead through areas owned by various government entities, such as the State of California and the National Park Service, having a public authority construct and own the tram may be the only method to secure rights-of-way.[15]

The remainder of the report was taken up by general plan maps showing the proposed route and existing topography, a longitudinal profile, and other maps that could be used in the planning of the project. As can be seen, the report was generally favorable to the project, but left a lot of concern for the estimated construction cost. Optimism remained high, though, that the project could be successfully undertaken. With the engineers' report in hand, and continued support from Palm Springs, the next order of business was to delve into the formation of the public authority recommended by the report and to begin securing financing.

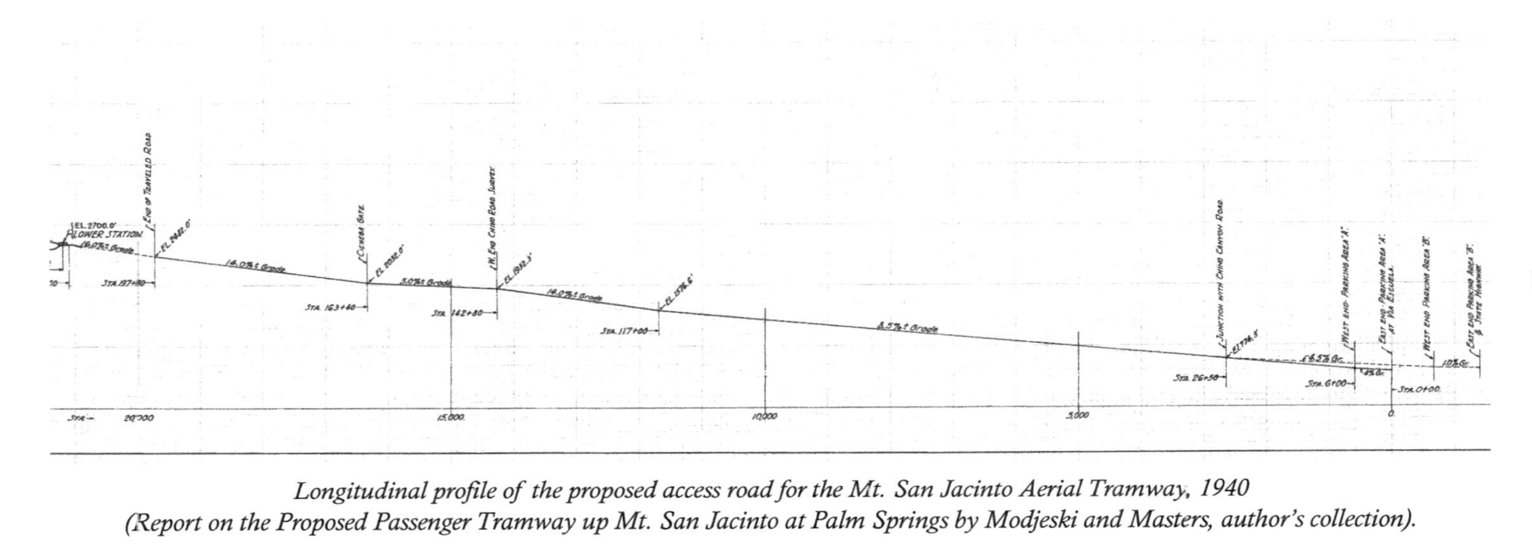

Longitudinal profile of the proposed access road for the Mt. San Jacinto Aerial Tramway, 1940
(Report on the Proposed Passenger Tramway up Mt. San Jacinto at Palm Springs by Modjeski and Masters, author's collection).

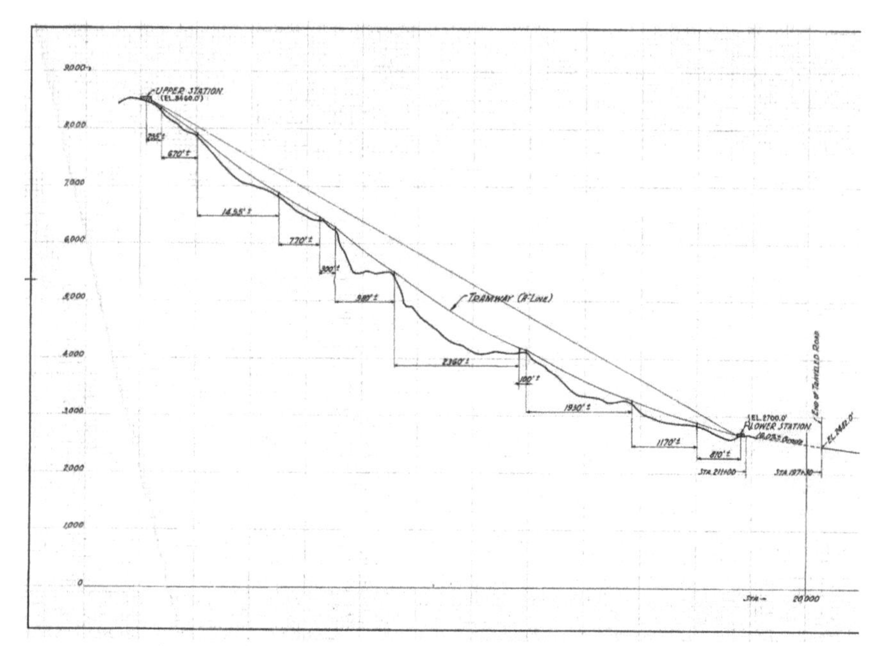

Longitudinal profile of the proposed Mt. San Jacinto Aerial Tramway, 1940 (Report on the Proposed Passenger Tramway up Mt. San Jacinto at Palm Springs by Modjeski and Masters, author's collection).

Signature block from the longitudinal profile of the proposed Mt. San Jacinto Aerial Tramway, 1940 (Report on the Proposed Passenger Tramway up Mt. San Jacinto at Palm Springs by Modjeski and Masters, author's collection).

PROPOSED
AERIAL PASSENGER TRAMWAY
UP
MT. SAN JACINTO
AT
PALM SPRINGS, CALIFORNIA

LONGITUDINAL PROFILE

SCALE IN FEET

1000 0 1000 2000

MODJESKI & MASTERS-ENG'RS.
RUSSEL G. CONE - ASSOC. ENG'R.
APRIL-1940.

Chapter 2 Endnotes

1. *The Desert Sun*, January 5, 1940.
2. *Ibid*, January 26, 1940.
3. In this era, traffic estimates were for the number of people thought to come to and use a facility such as the one proposed, NOT the number of car trips generated by a project as is the case today.
4. Modjeski and Masters. "Report on the Proposed Passenger Tramway up Mt. San Jacinto at Palm Springs, California." April, 1940, pp. 1-2.
5. *Ibid*, p. 1.
6. *Ibid*, p. 6.
7. *Ibid*, pp. 5-6.
8. It should be noted that any attempt at constructing the proposed project in Tahquitz Canyon would have meant obtaining permission and a right-of-way from the Agua Caliente Indians. While no mention is made of any such attempt, about ten years before, the backers of the Pines-to-Palms Highway had sought to run that route down Palm Canyon and into Palm Springs. This was met with adamant refusal by the Agua Calientes and there is little reason to assume that they would have been any more open to constructing a major transportation system in Tahquitz Canyon.
9. *Ibid*, p. 3.
10. *Ibid*, p. 4.
11. *Ibid*, pp. 11-12; http://www.usinflationcalculator.com/, accessed April 4, 2016. For a complete breakdown of the estimated cost, please see Appendix B.
12. Modjeski and Masters. "Report on the Proposed Passenger Tramway up Mt. San Jacinto at Palm Springs, California." April, 1940, pp. 11-12.
13. *Ibid*, pp. 15-18.
14. There will be more discussion on that in subsequent chapters.
15. Davis, August 1973, pp. 164-166.

Chapter 3

The Mt. San Jacinto Winter Park Authority

I am confident that with the progress made this year we will have the Tramway and in time to be a postwar construction job, ready for our guests when travel is unlimited again.

Harry Lockwood to The Desert Sun, *June 18, 1943.*

In order to address the dual issues of right-of-way acquisition and funding of the project, the next step for backers of the tramway plan was to create the necessary public authority recommended by the Modjeski and Masters report.

In effect, a public authority is a corporate instrument of the State that is created by the legislature to further public interests. It can be completely self-supporting (as this one would have to be) or operate with some state funds. Most importantly for the backers of the tramway, though, was that most authorities are authorized to issue bonds without voter approval to develop and maintain infrastructure, such as roads, toll roads, bridges, schools, and hospitals. Paying off the bonds is the responsibility of the public authority, and it is usually done with revenue income from the project.

In order to form a public authority, the backers of the tramway had to develop proposed legislation. Attorneys were sought, and throughout 1940, the legislation was developed with an eye toward the upcoming 1941 legislative session.[1] Luckily for the tramway's backers, the state legislature was set to meet during the first few months of 1941, so they had adequate time to draft their bills and find sponsors in the legislature. They found plenty of backing, so by January, 1941, two bills had been drafted and were ready for introduction into the State Legislature.

The two bills, SB 1051 and SB 1052, were nearly identical in most of their language. The bills, introduced into the California Senate on January 25, 1941, recognized the need for recreational facilities in the San Jacinto Mountains and indicated that it was,

> the policy of the State of California to foster and develop the greatest public use of the natural facilities of State parks

> and to provide for the acquisition, construction, completion, maintenance and operation of all works and property necessary or convenient therefore. There is in the State Park System Mount San Jacinto State Park, which is owned by the State and which is ideally situated for Winter sports, including skiing, tobogganing, sledding and skating, and which affords unlimited opportunities for healthful recreation in a snow area immediately adjacent to the desert recreational area of Palm Springs. These conditions are special and peculiar to this park and do not exist in any other park in the State Park System. Mount San Jacinto State Park is now practically inaccessible and in order to raise funds for its improvement and to make effective the purposes hereinabove declared, it is essential that a special authority be created to raise the necessary funds in the manner in this act.[2]

Both bills called for the creation of a new entity to be called the Palm Springs Winter Park Authority, and gave wide-ranging powers to that authority as to what could be done in the proposed area:

> The authority may acquire, construct or complete roads, highways, trams, tramways, aerial cableways, up-skis, ski-lifts, parking areas, skiing areas, areas for tobogganing, coasting, snowshoeing, sledding, ice skating, ski huts, hotels, pensions,[3] lodges, restaurants, buses, buildings, and all other works, properties and structures necessary, convenient or useful for the development of winter sports, and any other recreational facilities within the territorial limits of the authority . . . It may also acquire or construct and operate and maintain water supplies, and power and drainage systems, necessary, convenient, or useful to the project purposes of the authority . . . [4]

The main difference between the bills was in the makeup of the Authority. SB 1051's Authority would be one that would come under the purview of the city of Palm Springs by allowing cities within California to create parks or other recreational amenities outside of that city's limits. The bonds that could be sold under the Authority could be reimbursed through proceeds generated by the recreation facility (as opposed to being what are known as "general obligation" bonds). This method would work to Palm Springs' advantage because if the city was going to own the tramway, which the Mojeski report estimated would cost nearly $1.4 million, there was no way under existing finance law that Palm Springs as a city could expose itself to that kind of debt.[5]

By comparison, SB 1052 set up an Authority that would be a state agency, but rooted in Palm Springs. This type of Authority would be in effect a public corporation financed through the sale of bonds. This type of measure was not new to government operations during the Depression, as they allowed for more far-reaching improvements done under government auspices. In California, the Golden Gate Bridge and the Metropolitan Water District had both been established under this type of system, so it was reasoned that a tramway up and down Mt. San Jacinto could similarly be done. Unlike most of these previously-used Authorities, though, this proposed Palm Springs Winter Park Authority would only be sanctioned solely within Riverside County, as opposed to the entire State of California.[6]

The two bills went through the usual process of reading, re-reading, and even a few amendments during February, March, and April of 1941. By mid-April, SB 1052 had been passed and was ready for signature by Governor Culbert Olson. At this point, though, the bill and its proposals were becoming better known, and opposition began to mount. This opposition was rooted in the powers given the Winter Park Authority, though, and not against the tram itself. The proposed tram was known by many in the county – certainly Francis Crocker and his supporters had done their utmost to make their proposal known and appreciated. What raised objections was the perceived purposeful quiet treatment of the bill.

According to statements in the newspapers, members of the San Jacinto Mountain State Park Association[7] learned of SB 1052 and its provisions only around April 15 of 1941, and quickly called a meeting to discuss the bill. They immediately telegraphed their desire to have Governor Olson withhold his signature, at least for a while. "Nothing was known about the bill until the past few days, according to county and state park officials, and the bill . . . .is said to have been prepared by a firm of San Francisco lawyers without taking any of the county officials into consideration. . . . . Chairman Ralph W. Stanfield of the county supervisors expressed surprise when informed of the provisions of the bill."[8]

Over the next few days, members of the San Jacinto Mountain State Park Association, the Riverside County Board of Supervisors, and Riverside County District Attorney Earl Redwine all expressed reservations about the bill. These centered around the creation of an Authority that, as proposed, could encumber the entire County of Riverside with bonds that would affect only a small area of the County. In addition, there seems to have been no other local involvement in the creation of the bill beyond the City of Palm Springs – not the Riverside County Board of Supervisors, other cities, or State agencies. An unnamed member of the State Park Association stated it bluntly, "the bill seems to be an attempt to grab control of the entire mountain by Palm Springs interests to the detriment of Riverside County as a whole."[9] Similarly, Supervisor Ed Hill thought that the bill would create "a little dictatorship in the county." John Phillips, the sponsor of the bill, countered by talking about the benefits of having such a project in Riverside County. He finished by saying he "cannot understand [the] sudden flurry of opposition against the bill, which has been continuously discussed for more than two months."[10]

On April 30, the Riverside County Board of Supervisors held a hearing to discuss the bill, which had already been approved by both houses of the legislature and was simply awaiting the Governor's signature. During the meeting, Supervisor Edward Talbot from Perris, whose 5th district included the San Jacinto Mountain area, asked "why wasn't the board of supervisors given this power instead of the city council of Palm Springs? Not any of the area [slated for construction of the tramway] is within the confines of the city. It is a county function. This whole bill doesn't show good faith; it is a direct slap at the board of supervisors."[11]

At the end of the meeting, the Board of Supervisors voted 4-1 to send a letter to Governor Olson asking that he veto the bill. Supervisor Robert Dillon of Banning, in whose district both Palm Springs and the area to be incorporated into the tramway fell, was the lone opponent. The basis of the Board's letter involved five points:

1. The powers of the bill are too broad;
2. The exemption from taxation of the revenue bonds to finance the project is objectionable to the board;
3. The territorial jurisdiction of the authority is too extensive;

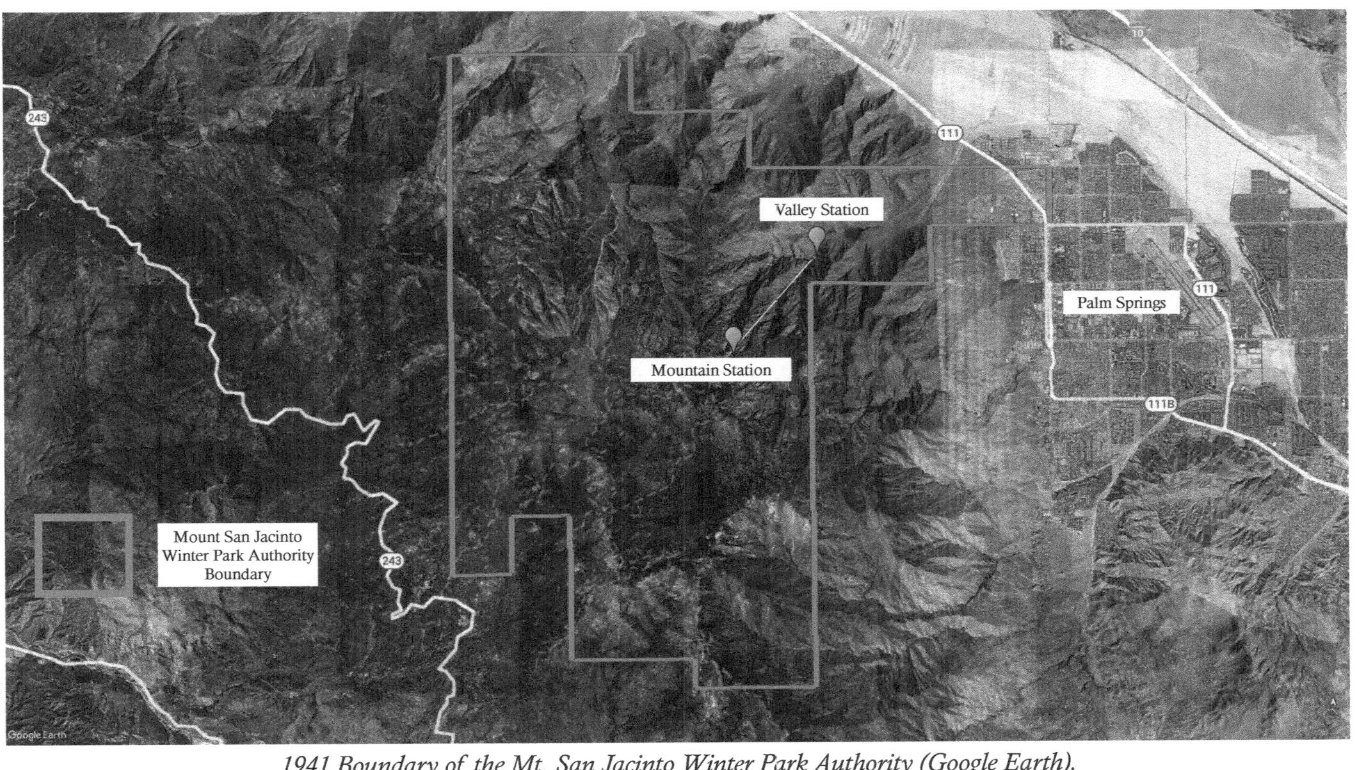

1941 Boundary of the Mt. San Jacinto Winter Park Authority (Google Earth).
NOTE - Location of Tramway for reference purposes only.

4. The rights of eminent domain are unwarranted and contrary to public policy, and;
5. Privately owned property would be unduly burdened.[12]

As can been seen, the opposition to the bill did not in any way have to do with construction of the tramway itself. In fact, during the various meetings, even stalwart opponents like Supervisor Talbot indicated that he had no issue with the tram, just the points listed above as they pertained to the creation of the proposed Palm Springs Winter Park Authority. In a last-minute attempt to explain the opposition was not about the tram itself, Supervisor Robert Dillon sent his own telegram to the Governor explaining just this fact.

In the end, the opposition won the day. On May 12, 1941, Governor Olson vetoed SB 1052. He objected to the broad authority given the City of Palm Springs, which would be able to appoint a board of five people who would have jurisdiction over such a large area of wilderness not within the city itself. In addition,

> this absolute grant of jurisdiction and control over a large segment of the scenic resources of the state without any control or supervision by the state park commission to which the people have delegated the responsibility of providing wise development of these resources is a step to which I can not consent. San Jacinto state park is a part of California's state park system paid for with public funds. If its development should be delegated to a body other than the state park commission, then any use of state park property by such independent body should only be granted subject to approval of the commission.

That said, he agreed with the concept of making the park more accessible to the public, "but at the same time, the natural beauties and the primitive conditions in a large part of the park can be preserved."[13]

At this point, backers of the tramway still had a way out. SB 1051 had been tabled for a few months. It had essentially the same language as SB 1052, except for the makeup of the Authority. Sen. John Phillips basically took SB 1052, cut and pasted its language into SB 1051, but this time had the 5-member Authority consist of two ex officio state officers (the Director of Natural Resources and the Chairman of the

State Park Commission), two members appointed by the City of Palm Springs, and one member appointed by the County of Riverside. It was thought that this new provision would remove most of the Supervisors' objections, and that they and others would support it.

SB 1051 was passed by the California State Senate on June 6, followed by approval by the Assembly on June 14. However, despite the approvals of both houses of the legislature, Governor Olson refused to sign this new bill, and it died due to lack of signature. In a brief statement, Governor Olson indicated that not all of his objections to SB 1052 had been addressed, further stating that "the bill is not in the best interests of all the people" of the State of California since the Authority was still controlled by members of Palm Springs and Riverside County.[14] Due to the amount of hard work that had been put into the effort to secure a Winter Park Authority, *The Desert Sun* seemed resigned to the death of the project, stating that, "since it will be two years before a bill can again be introduced, it is believed that the project, which would have meant the spending of millions of dollars in this county, is killed for all time."[15]

As we know, the project was far from dead, although it did take a hiatus at this time due to much larger events happening worldwide. It was realized that little progress could be made in construction during this time, but as the war progressed, the aerial tramway proposal was brought up again, this time not only as a recreational amenity but also as a post-war construction and employment project to help stave off the certain recession and unemployment period that would naturally result from the end of the war. In late 1942, Henry Lockwood, the attorney who had been representing the proposal, was again secured to begin anew the effort to form a winter park authority.

After a series of meetings with proponents of the tramway project, county officials, and others including various chambers of commerce, a new plan for the project was developed for the 1943 legislative session. Most of the provisions of the original bills pertaining to the actual tramway were kept – what was altered was some of the other provisions regarding the scope of the proposed Palm Springs Winter Park Authority. The first of these provisions was the elimination of several sections of land on the west slope of the San Jacinto Mountains, mainly above and to the north of Idyllwild. In addition, the powers of eminent domain were severely curtailed. Finally, limits were placed on housing in the proposal so that only that housing needed for emergency shelter could be constructed. A new bill, incorporating these and a few other minor amendments, was agreed to by the Board of Supervisors at their meeting of April 19, 1943.[16]

The next day, Assemblyman Nelson Dilworth of Hemet introduced AB 2001 into the legislature to again approve the creation of the Palm Springs Winter Park Authority. This bill, with lots of backing both in Riverside County and Sacramento, sailed through the Assembly and was approved on April 28, 1943 with a vote of 59 – 5.[17] In turn, it went to the Senate where it passed on May 8 by a vote of 28-2.[18]

At this point, it was up to a new Governor, Earl Warren, to sign the bill. Governor Warren received several petitions and telegrams over the next several weeks urging him to sign the Tramway Bill as it was called. As time went on, speculation mounted as to why the Governor was not signing the bill, noting that he had until June 9 to do so. Just a few days before the deadline, *The Desert Sun* lamented,

> The big question in the minds of leading Palm Springs citizens today is: What is staying the hand of Governor Earl Warren on the bill to create the Palm Springs Winter Park Authority? . . . . .
> The measure creating the Palm Springs Winter Park authority is a post-war measure. It is designed to provide employment which will be sorely needed after the war is concluded in victory. It will pave the way for the construction of a spectacular aerial tramway, which will whisk people from the floor of the desert to winter playgrounds, second to none in the nation. All Southern California will benefit by its construction. It will be the leading tourist attraction in a section replete with tourist attractions.[19]

June 9 came and went without a signature, killing the bill via a pocket veto. The only reason given from Governor Warren's office was to say that "it was contrary to state park policy in granting control to local agencies over park facilities."[20]

Although little could be ascertained at the time as to whether the drive would continue, few doubted that it wouldn't. By late 1944, it was time to prepare for the 1945 legislative session and backers of the bill were busy lining up more allies to support their proposal. In late December, 1944, Francis Crocker, Culver Nichols, and Walter Kofelt met

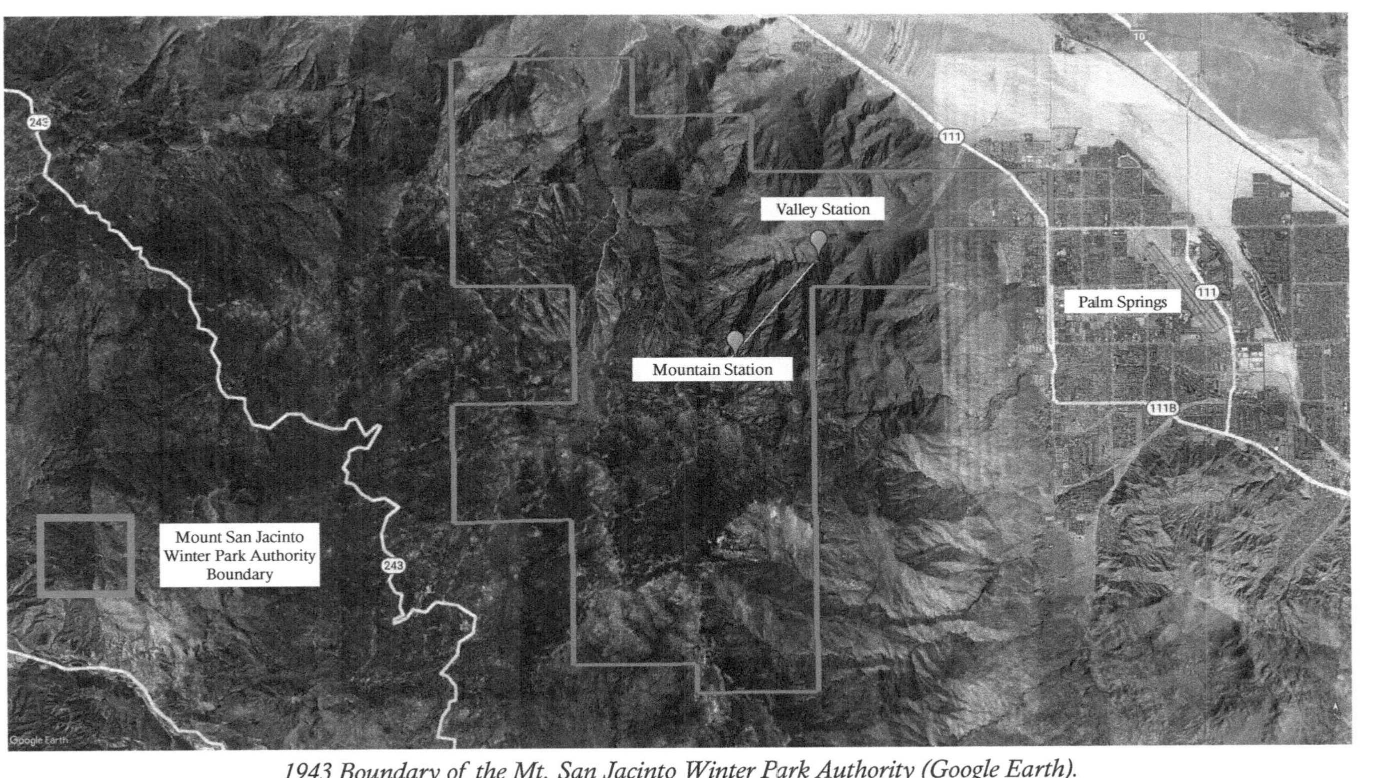

1943 Boundary of the Mt. San Jacinto Winter Park Authority (Google Earth).
NOTE - Location of Tramway for reference purposes only.

with high-ranking officials of the California State Chamber of Commerce. After going over the proposed tramway with them in a two-hour meeting, Crocker and his cohorts came away with the support of the Chamber of Commerce. Then, in a stroke of luck, the California State Park Commission was due to hold its regular monthly meeting in Palm Springs in January, 1945. On January 4, the Commission met at the Desert Inn, and on their docket was the proposed tramway. At the meeting, Francis Crocker again spoke for the project, and he and others outlined the many benefits they had been championing for nearly 10 years. They also indicated that the tramway would be a post-war project paid for not by State taxpayers but by the passengers riding the tram itself. The bill to create the Winter Park Authority was necessary so that contracts could be entered into with both the Federal and State governments to allow construction and operation of the project into the Mt. San Jacinto State Park. Finally, they indicated that their principle objective was not actually to make money off of the tram but to construct a means of accessing the higher elevations of the San Jacinto Mountains for the purpose of having a winter sports area. This latter position was important for recreational needs that would be more and more necessary as the population of Southern California boomed.[21]

The newest version of the legislation, which was only slightly updated from the 1943 version, was introduced into the legislature by the newest Assemblyman from Riverside County, Phillip Boyd, who had been mayor of Palm Springs. Introduced into the State Assembly on January 25th as AB 1239, the new bill removed State officers as members of the Authority and revised its membership to include two members appointed by Palm Springs, another two members by the Riverside County Board of Supervisors, and three members appointed by the Governor of California. Additionally, all property, title, and income would be vested in the Authority only and not with the City of Palm Springs, County of Riverside, or State of California. To ward off any confusion as to whether the Authority was a Palm Springs entity, the proposed name of the Authority was changed to the Mount San Jacinto Winter Park Authority.

The bill went through the normal procedures, with some small amendments regarding financial considerations made. Assemblyman Boyd seemed very optimistic of its passing throughout the process, and in fact on May 25, 1945, the State Assembly passed AB 1239 on a unanimous 61-0 vote.[22]

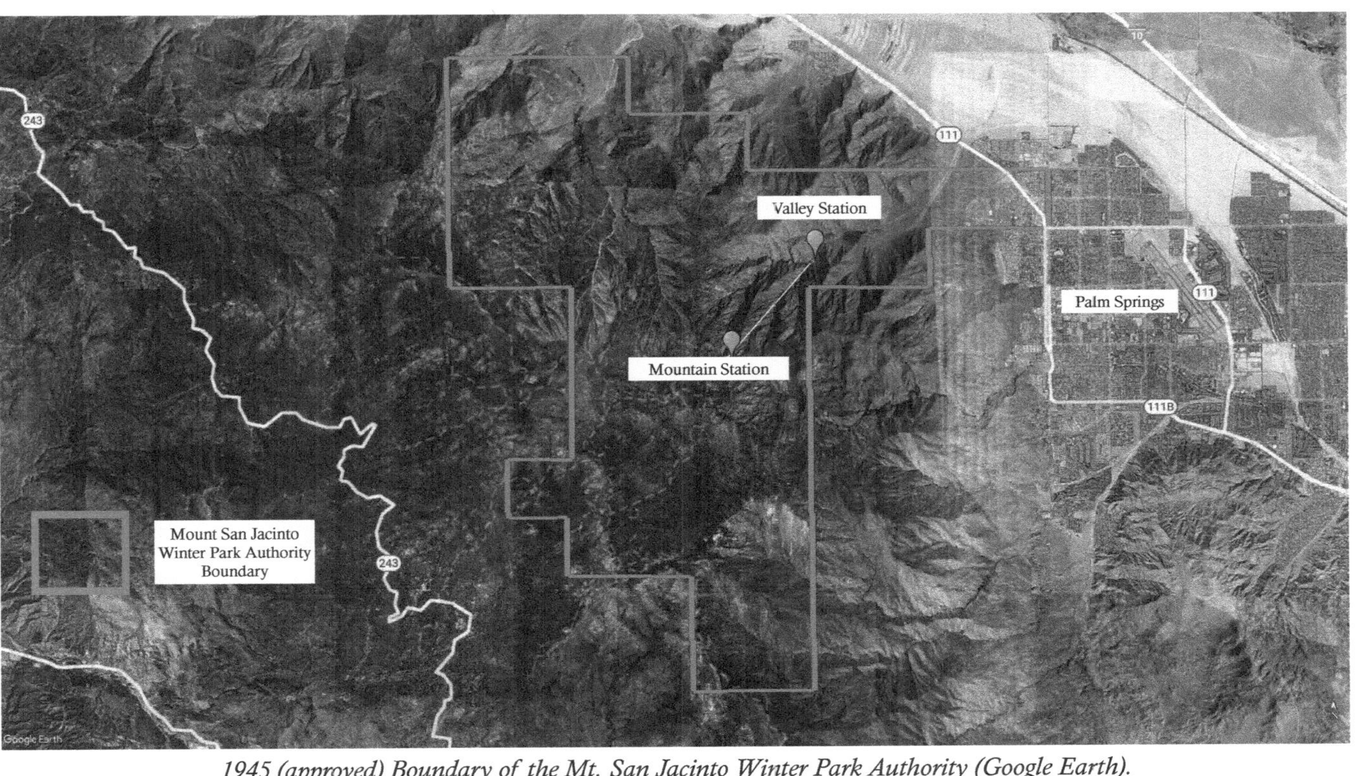

1945 (approved) Boundary of the Mt. San Jacinto Winter Park Authority (Google Earth).
NOTE - Location of Tramway for reference purposes only.

Governor Earl Warren signs the act creating the Mt. San Jacinto Winter Park Authority, June 25, 1945. Standing left to right are Phillip Boyd, Francis Crocker, and Nelson Dilworth (Palm Springs Historical Society photo).

The bill then went to the State Senate where it was passed by a vote of 39-1 on June 11.[23] This time, there was little waiting and anxiety before the Governor signed the bill. Governor Earl Warren's signature was affixed to the bill on June 25, 1945, and a major milestone towards the creation of the Palm Springs Aerial Tramway was finished.[24]

In the minds of many, the creation of the Mt. San Jacinto Winter Park Authority all but ensured the eventual construction of the aerial tramway. Sure, there would be much administrative work ahead – surveys, more calculations, bond approvals and sales – but the idea of Palm Springs having a unique attraction like the tram in its own backyard seemed at the time a done deal. It had had much support both locally and at the state level, and seemingly the only opposition to it was in regard to the powers initially vested with the Authority, not the actual tram itself. In fact, for the first 10 years of the existence of the aerial tramway proposal, the only meaningful opposition to it came in the form of opposition to the powers and extent of the Mt. San Jacinto Winter Park Authority. Although there were some voices who expressed opposition to it based upon injecting human development into a pristine area, those voices were small, not unified, and given little credence. Before we delve into the main opposition to the tramway from the environmental standpoint, it is necessary to examine efforts to preserve various aspects of the San Jacinto Mountains throughout the late 19th and early 20th centuries so that a better understanding of the opposition can be had.

Chapter 3 Endnotes

1. During this time, the California Legislature met for the first few months of the odd-numbered years.
2. California Legislature, S. B. 1051, 54th session (1941).
3. In this sense, a pension is an older term meaning "a boarding house in France and other European countries, providing full or partial board at a fixed rate."
4. California Legislature, S. B. 1051, 54th session (1941).
5. California cities at the time could incur no more than 15% of their assessed valuation in debt. In 1940, that assessed valuation was $7,258,000, which meant that Palm Springs could incur no more than $1,088,700 in debt, which was nearly $300,000 less than the total projected cost of the tram (Davis, August 1973, pp. 166-167).
6. California Legislature, S. B. 1052, 54th session (1941); Davis, August 1973, pp. 167-173.
7. The San Jacinto Mountain State Park Association was incorporated on September 22, 1928 to "further resource preservation, as a part of the scientific, conservation, scenic and educational values of the parks. The association, along with the Riverside County Chamber of Commerce and other organizations and individuals, sponsored many "show me" trips for the press, government people, conservationists, and others who might help the cause." (https://msjnha.org/history/ - Website of the Mt. San Jacinto Natural History Association, accessed May 30, 2020).
8. Riverside *Daily Press*, April 26, 1941.
9. *Ibid.*
10. *Ibid.*
11. Riverside *Daily Press*, April 30, 1941.
12. Riverside *Daily Press*, May 1, 1941.
13. Riverside *Daily Press*, May 12, 1941.
14. Palm Springs *Limelight*, August 7, 1941.
15. *The Desert Sun*, July 25, 1941. Again, at this time, the State Legislature met from January to April of the odd-numbered years.
16. Riverside *Daily Press*, April 20, 1943.
17. *The Desert Sun*, April 30, 1943.
18. *The Desert Sun*, May 14, 1943.
19. *The Desert Sun*, June 4, 1943.
20. *The Desert Sun*, June 11, 1943.
21. *The Desert Sun*, January 5, 1945.

22. *The Desert Sun*, June 1, 1945.

23. *The Desert Sun*, June 15, 1945; Davis, August 1973, p. 191. The one dissenting vote was Senator Arthur Breed Jr. of Alameda County. Senator Breed's father, Arthur Breed Sr., had written the state park system enabling acts of 1927.

24. There were a total of three legislative attempts to form the Mt. San Jacinto Winter Park Authority. However, there was a fourth and earlier attempt at the tramway itself. In 1939, the American Funicular Corporation submitted an application for a right-of-way to the U. S. Forest Service, which was summarily rejected for numerous reasons. Often, articles will indicate that attempts to build the Palm Springs Aerial Tramway date to 1939, but in actuality, it is 1941 when the true attempts began.

Chapter 4

Development of Open Space in the San Jacinto Mountains

Those who know Mount San Jacinto and the surrounding country will join enthusiastically with citizens of Riverside and recommend that charmed district to the newly created State Park Board for consideration as the site for a state park. . . . If there are to be state parks in Southern California, and there surely should be, Mt. San Jacinto deserves to be listed amongst the first sites to be considered.

Editorial, Los Angeles Express, *January 3, 1928.*

For as long as people have lived in the Southern California region, they have used the San Jacinto Mountains for many purposes, including food, shelter, and as a way of escaping the heat of the desert. Beginning in the 1870s, as non-native people began to pour into the region, privately-run camp sites and resorts sprang up to allow people to enjoy the mountains in every level of comfort. With this influx, though, came the ongoing issue of resource development as logging interests entered the region also and clear-cut the old-growth forests for buildings to house the burgeoning population. In the 1800s, as the vast area that was the western United States was opening up to the influx of Americans, many of these Americans saw the resources that the West had to offer as so incalculably large that they would never be used up. These resources could never be exhausted, so the thinking went, and they were there for the taking.

But by the post-Civil War era, though, many people were decrying what they considered to be the wanton, exploitative, destruction of forests throughout the country for immediate gains. Thus began some twenty years of policy debates on many levels. These debates, and the efforts of many people, eventually led to the Forest Reserve Act of 1891, which established the means to protect wooded areas as Federal "forest reserves" to be managed by the Department of the Interior. The Act was signed into law by President Benjamin Harrison on March 3, 1891, and within the next two years, four Forest Reserves were created in California – the Sierra, San Gabriel, San Bernardino, and Trabuco.[1]

Campers enjoying the mountains at "Idlewild," c. 1890s
(Idyllwild Area Historical Society).

Although the San Jacinto Mountains were conspicuously left out of these initial four Reserves, it would not be for long. In 1896, the U.S. Department of the Interior created the National Forest Commission which was charged with exploring and inspecting America's various timberlands to ascertain whether they should be preserved and/or protected. During the Commission's trip through Southern California, with none other than John Muir as a guide, they toured the San Jacinto Mountains and reported favorably on that range's potential as a forest. Based upon this recommendation, President Grover Cleveland signed the bill creating the San Jacinto Forest Reserve on February 22, 1897.[2]

While these early forest reserves sounded like a good idea and had good intentions, the reality was that they were established with little to no enforcement capabilities. In many instances, logging and other activities continued. Upon learning that many of the Forest Reserves were still being exploited, the Federal Government eventually added teams of forest rangers to help enforce forest regulations in these Forest Reserves.

In early 1907, all of the Forest Reserves nationwide were changed to National Forests, with the San Jacinto National Forest being one of the larger ones. The existence of the San Jacinto National Forest under that name, though, lasted only about one year. In the summer of 1908, President Theodore Roosevelt combined the San Jacinto Na-

View of the San Jacinto Mountains from Santa Rosa Peak (Author photo).

tional Forest and the Trabuco National Forest into one entity and renamed it the Cleveland National Forest for the late President Grover Cleveland. This name change did not sit well with locals, but the name stuck as it still does today for the portion of the Santa Ana Mountains between Riverside and Orange Counties. Further change came in 1925 when the San Jacinto Mountains portion of the Cleveland National Forest was removed and added to the San Bernardino National Forest, a move that remains in effect today. Because of the chosen route of the Palm Springs Aerial Tramway, which would cross lands encompassed by the San Jacinto portion of the San Bernardino National Forest, backers would have to appeal to the U. S. Government for portions of their eventual approvals.

The creation of National Forests was only the first of many ways interested parties sought to protect some or all of the forested lands of the San Jacinto Mountains. In the summer of 1907, Dr. Walter Lindley, a physician from Los Angeles and consummate booster of Southern California's climate, wrote a letter to the editor of the *Hemet News* saying that he had seen deer in the San Jacinto Mountains, and not that much later, hunters:

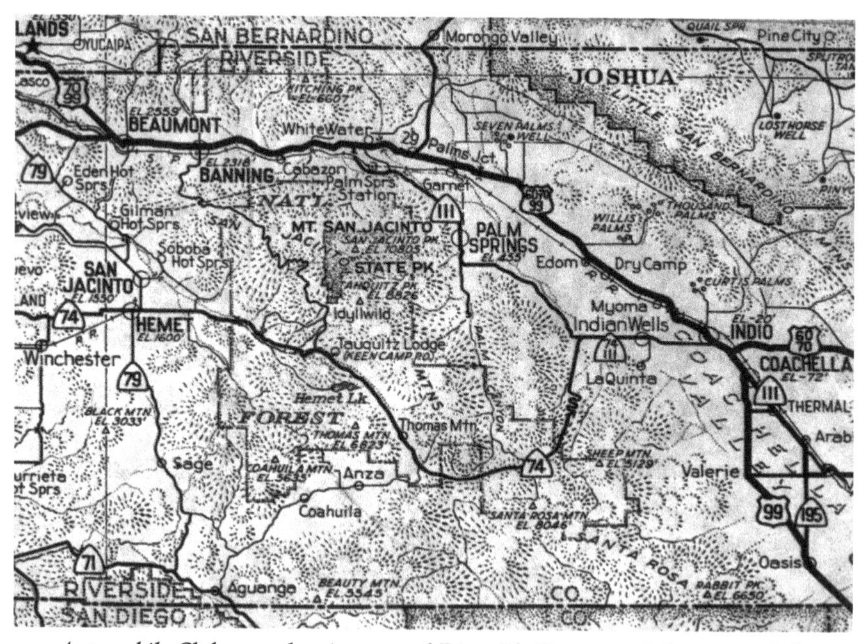

Automobile Club map showing central Riverside County and the extent of the San Jacinto District of the San Bernardino National Forest c. 1938 (Automobile Club of Southern California Archives).

Riverside (has) in the San Jacinto mountains the most beautiful natural park in California outside of the Yosemite Valley. With the protection of the Riverside county supervisors and the federal forest rangers it would be possible to have the deer in these mountain so plentiful that it would be a sight that people would travel far to witness. . . . . on my way up the mountain, eight horsemen from Redlands passed the stage with their guns and equipment . . . .Do the people of Riverside county propose to allow this to go on year after year until, like the antelope, the deer will be simply a memory?[3]

Dr. Walter Lindley (Internet photo).

On another front, a year after Dr. Lindley's editorial, Harold Marshall, the San Jacinto forest supervisor, proposed creating a "Tahquitz Peak and Palm Canyon National Monument" centered around the two named locations. That proposal, which would have combined areas of both the mountains and nearby deserts, died quickly when Associate U. S. Forester Overton Price wrote a response saying, "there does not seem to be anything of any unusual scientific or historical interest connected with the lands in question."[4]

The next proposal to preserve some of the San Jacintos came from Riverside County Superintendent of Schools Raymond Cree, an ardent nature lover, outdoorsman, and supporter of preservation. In 1917, Cree developed the idea of setting aside a huge swath of land ranging from San Jacinto Peak to Palm Canyon to the Salton Sea. This time, the large area proposed for preservation would be set aside as a national monument, the only one in Southern California. Unfortunately for Cree, when he took his idea formally to the Riverside County Board of Supervisors, they indicated that the proposed area to be set aside was too large, and asked that it be trimmed. Like so many ideas, though, this one faded out at the time due to the onset of America's involvement in World War I.[5]

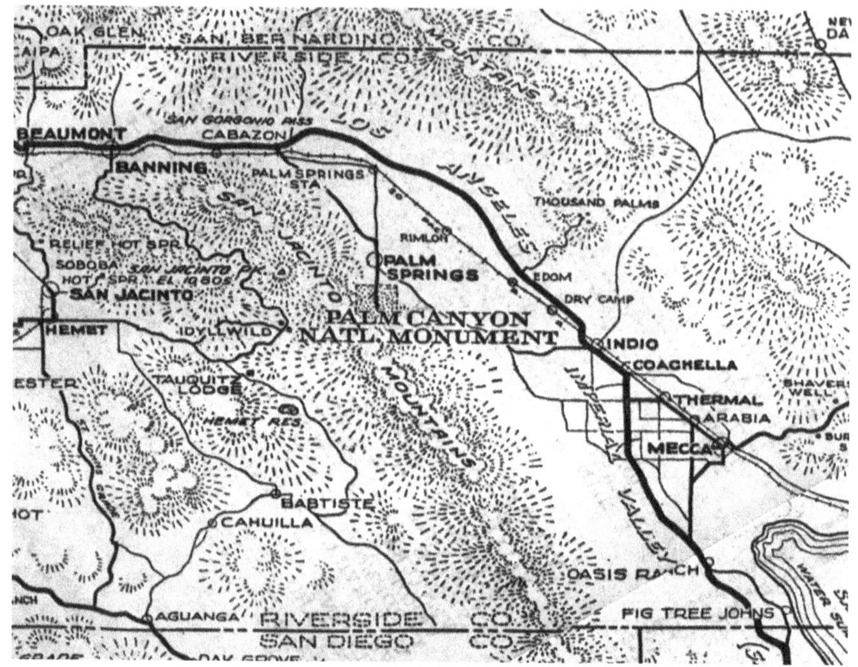

Automobile Club map showing central Riverside County and the location of the proposed Palm Canyon National Monument c. 1920 (Automobile Club of Southern California Archives).

Cree's idea for a national monument would only be on hiatus for two years, for in 1919, in the aftermath of World War I, the Board of Supervisors was looking for a monument to set aside to remember the roughly 100 Riverside County men who had died during that war. To make this happen, the Board appointed another ardent conservationist, Arthur Lovekin, to develop a plan. His plan was to set aside not only San Jacinto Peak but also Palm and Andreas Canyons in a memorial/park. Unfortunately, the U. S. Forest Service refused to have any of its territory in such a park, and so the idea of including San Jacinto Peak had to be dropped.

Undeterred, Lovekin enlisted the help of Mission Inn owner Frank Miller to aide in getting the support of Steven Mather, the National Park Service's director. At a meeting at the Mission Inn, Mather was warm to the idea, but suggested that perhaps a National Monument might be a better way to develop this idea.[6]

Lovekin and his allies persevered, and in January, 1920, U. S. Representative William Kettner introduced a bill to create Palm Canyon National Monument. While this proposal had a lot of support, one key group had been left out of the planning efforts – the Agua Caliente Indians. They owned much of the lands that were slated for inclusion in the new monument, and without their consent, the bill eventually died. Two years later, hoping to keep the momentum going and also hoping to bring the Agua Caliente around, Lovekin again had Riverside County's new representative, Phil Swing, introduce a similar bill creating a national monument, only this time including wording that would make the creation incumbent upon the approval of the Agua Caliente. The Agua Caliente, though, were steadfast in their refusal to hand over their land for any use beyond their own, and the idea of a National Monument encompassing Palm Canyon died.

Another person interested in preserving a portion of the San Jacintos entered the picture at roughly the same time as Art Lovekin. Itinerant writer George Law, who was based out of Los Angeles but had a summer home at a place he called "Caramba" on the east face of the San Jacinto Mountains, submitted petitions in 1917 to create a "National Deer Park" on the east face of the mountain. Law and others had been alarmed at the fact that the State of California in 1915 had set aside huge game reserves in the San Gabriel and San Bernardino Mountains, leaving the San Jacinto Mountains, in their minds, wide open to bands of hunters who would wipe out most if not all of the game within two seasons. Law's proposal had two tracks. One was the creation of the National Deer Park deer breeding ground " . . . . to insure [sic] a perpetual supply of deer and other game." The second was to create the National Deer Park in an effort to circumvent the proposals for national monument status;

Tinted postcard view of Palm Canyon by Stephen Willard, 1920s (Author's collection).

"For scenic reasons, this region is deserving of being made into a National Park; but this would hardly be possible. However, setting it aside for the deer will accomplish the preservation of its scenic value also."[7]

Law's idea took hold, and in 1922, Phil Swing introduced a bill into Congress to create the "Tahquitz National Game Preserve," the name being radically altered from "National Deer Park." Swing's bill did not make it through congress, but four years later, it was altered and reintroduced and this time was passed. On July 3, 1926, President Calvin Coolidge signed the bill to create the "Tahquitz National Game Preserve."[8]

Unfortunately for backers of the Preserve, the bill had a fatal flaw which was either overlooked or not considered. The bill called for all of the land within the proposed boundaries of the Preserve to be under the auspices of the United States (i.e. within the National Forest). The Southern Pacific Railroad, though, owned a large amount of property within the proposed area in a checkerboard pattern.[9] Negotiations with the Southern Pacific proved fruitless as no agreement could be reached on either swapping land with the railroad or coming up with the needed funds to buy the land.

Instead of continuing a futile fight with the mighty Southern Pacific Railroad, backers of a proposed game preserve decided to try the same approach but at the state level. Backers took their proposal to State officials and the State Legislature twice, in 1925 and 1927. The second attempt was successful, and on May 17, 1927, Governor C. C. Young of California signed into law the creation of the Tahquitz State Game Refuge which encompassed 30 square miles surrounding San Jacinto Peak and portions to the southeast including Tahquitz Peak. A game preserve in the San Jacinto Mountains had finally been realized.[10]

These latter attempts at preservation in the San Jacinto Mountains meant that wildlife in the region would be protected and hunting would be curtailed if not totally banned, but made no provision for preservation of the land itself. While deer and other animals would be protected, there was nothing stopping further development of the higher regions in the form of private homes, commercial buildings, or even highways. In fact, throughout the 1920s, there were many calls for construction of a road and/or highway from Idyllwild north to San Jacinto Peak.[11]

As the 1920s wore on, it became more and more apparent to several people that some over-arching method of preserving some if not all of the San Jacinto Mountains would have to be enacted before it was too late. Competing interests both at the State and Federal levels meant that there would be corresponding competing attempts to accomplish this. Luckily, this time, they worked.

On the federal side, the 1920s saw the development of a mind set in the Forest Service that advocated for the preservation of what was termed "wilderness lands." These wilderness lands, it was reasoned, should be set aside and maintained in a wilderness state, i.e. free of much human interference. The most influential advocate for this was Aldo Leopold, who is today considered by many to be the father of wildlife ecology and the United States' wilderness system. A conservationist, forester, philosopher, educator, writer, and outdoor enthusiast, Leopold is best known for his promotion of what he called the "land ethic," which calls for an ethical, caring relationship between people and nature.[12]

> The last word in ignorance is the man who says of an animal or plant, "What good is it?" If the land mechanism as a whole is good, then every part is good, whether we understand it or not. If the biota, in the course of eons, has built something we like but do not understand, then who but a fool would discard seemingly useless parts? To keep every cog and wheel is the first precaution of intelligent tinkering.[13]

Leopold was employed as a forester in Albuquerque at the time, and was able to use his position to advocate for wilderness preservation. By 1926, his ideas had reached the highest ranks of the Forest Service, and in that year, William B. Greeley, the Chief Forester of the United States, called upon all of the national forest supervisors under him to develop a list of lands to be considered for wilderness status.

The San Bernardino Forest Supervisor at the time was Steven A. Nash-Boulden. When he received the directive to propose areas for conservation, he submitted a list advocating for areas within the San Gabriel, San Bernardino, and Santa Rosa Mountains, but conspicuously not the San Jacinto Mountains. Regardless, the effort of Greeley and others seems to have stalled at this point.

On the State side, however, proposals to save part if not all of the San Jacinto Mountains were just gaining steam. Efforts to start a California State park system had begun in the mid-1920s. By the end of

Photo postcard view of Tahquitz Peak from Saunders Meadow, San Jacinto Mountains, by E. B. Gray, 1920s (Author's collection).

1927, a Joint Parks Committee, formed in Los Angeles, was proposing several areas in Southern California for State park status, since the only state parks at the time were all in Northern California. On November 28 of that year, they appealed to the Riverside County Board of Supervisors for input, and they eagerly agreed to join the effort, appointing a committee chaired by Arthur Lovekin to develop a list of potential state park sites in Riverside County.[14]

By the end of January, 1928, many people throughout Riverside County were in agreement with the idea of setting aside a large area around and containing Mt. San Jacinto as a state park. On January 26, the Riverside County Board of Forestry met and enthusiastically endorsed the idea. A permanent committee was then authorized to develop and push the proposal.[15]

This group, soon named the Mt. San Jacinto State Park Association, spent 1928 discussing the creation of a state park surrounding Mt. San Jacinto. Hikes, horseback outings, and other "show me" trips were conducted during the summer, and every chance offered was given over to extolling the virtues of the region and its potential as a state park. This effort was bolstered in November, 1928, when the residents of California voted in a $6 million bond[16] specifically for purchasing state parks.

When it appeared as though a concrete plan was underway at the state level to preserve the San Jacinto Mountains, efforts by the Federal Government began again in earnest. Seeing a mounting effort to create a state park, San Bernardino National Park supervisor Stephen A. Nash-Boulden put forth another proposal, this one to set aside a 34-square mile area generally around the Tahquitz State Game Refuge as a roadless wilderness area. With this new proposal, it now looked as if there would be a competition for control of the San Jacinto Mountains between the National Forest Service and the State of California which wanted to create a state park.[17] Hoping to avert a major crisis and ending up with a hodge-podge of competing interests, the California State Park Commission tried to stave off the confusion by hiring Newton Drury, a UC Berkeley literature professor and officer in the Save the Redwoods League, to act as go-between and negotiate an agreement between the Federal and State governments.

In the end, after months of back-and-forth negotiations, Drury, who had ties to all of the entities involved, was able to effect an agreement that was in all of the landholders' best interests.

In essence, the plan involved a three-way land deal as follows: The U. S. Forest Service would give the Southern Pacific Railroad a roughly 24-square mile rectangle of land including San Jacinto peak and sections to both the east and west of it. In turn, the Southern Pacific would deed to the U. S. Forest Service 12 square miles of land located outside of that rectangle. The California State Park Commission would then enter the agreement by purchasing the 24-square mile rectangle from the Southern Pacific Railroad.

Western view from Santa Rosa Peak (Author's photo).

Map indicating the 3-way land transfer that created Mt. San Jacinto State Park. The area in blue represents lands given to the Southern Pacific Railroad by the U. S. Forest Service, which in turn were purchased by the California State Park Commission to create the State Park. The areas in red were given to the U. S. Forest Service by the Southern Pacific Railroad (Google Earth maps).

On February 26, 1930, Newton Drury presented his plan to the Riverside-based Mt. San Jacinto State Park Association, which gave it a half-hearted endorsement because they thought it didn't go far enough. Drury won over the Association when he assured them that the proposal would be added to in years to come. Afterwards, a series of meetings was held throughout the spring of 1930 in which the benefits of the proposed deal were touted. This culminated on July 9, when the California State Park Commission met in Idyllwild to make a formal recommendation. At that meeting, the three parties all agreed to the plan, and the prospect of having both State and Federal wilderness areas in the San Jacinto Mountains was on its way to completion. In a printed statement, L. A. Barrett and Newton Drury stated that,

> The San Jacinto Mountain State Park will be maintained as a wilderness area. No roads or buildings will be permitted although an excellent system of trails will be constructed.[18]

A week later, the Hemet *News* explained to its readers,

> **Wilderness in Fact** – Primitive yet, the promise is made by the authorities that it shall always remain so, a bit of unspoiled nature for unborn generations to come and enjoy; a place where the wheels that carry man almost everywhere can find no road, where the honk of autos and the putt-putt of exploding gasoline will never disturb those in search of recreation and rest.[19]

The projected price for enacting this agreement was $84,218.75. Of that, half would come from the state park bonds that had been recently passed, $40,000 would come from Riverside County, and the remaining funds (just over $2,000) would be supplied by the Mt. San Jacinto State Park Association.

While the State Park petitions were winding their way through the echelons of government, ultimately to be approved by the State Legislature, the Federal Government was proceeding with its own plans to preserve their portions of the San Jacinto Mountains.

In July, 1929, the U. S. Forest Service issued what was termed Regulation L-20. This policy, which was neither mandate nor law, defined among other things "primitive areas" and what could and

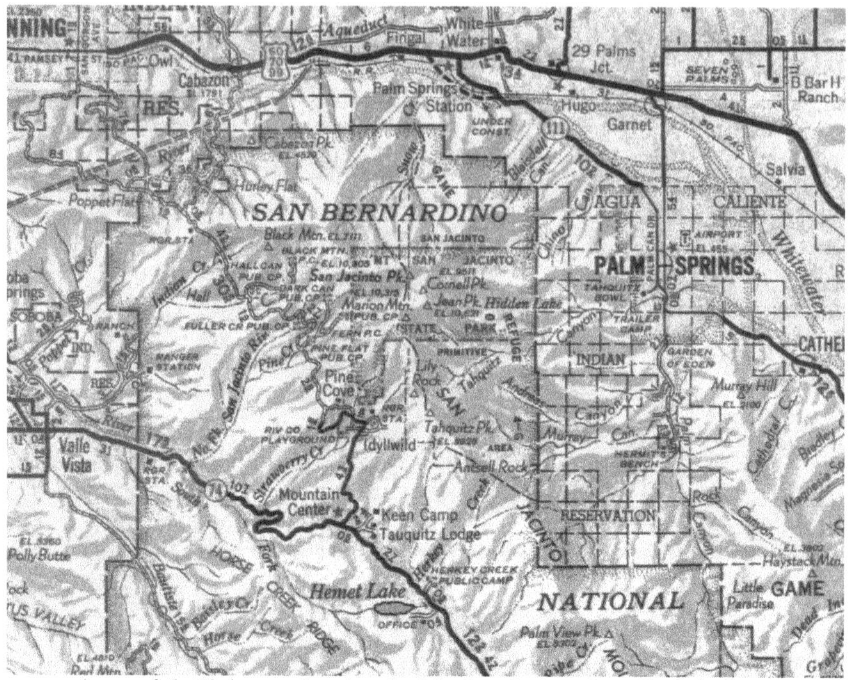

Automobile Club map showing the Mt. San Jacinto State Park (red) and the San Jacinto Primitive Area to the Park's north and south, c. 1945 (Automobile Club of Southern California Archives).

could not be done in them. According to Regulation L-20, the Forest Service was to set aside "a series of areas to be known as primitive areas, and within which, to the extent of the Department's authority, will be maintained primitive conditions of environment, transportation, habitation, and subsistence, with a view to conserving the value of such areas for purposes of public education, inspiration, and recreation."[20]

In 1930, the U. S. Forest Service submitted paperwork to their Washington D. C. office to begin their approval process. Within the package was a letter dated October 1, 1930, stating that, "If this transaction goes through, it is the plan of the State Park Commission to maintain their lands as a part of the combined San Jacinto Mountain State Park–Forest Service Primitive Area of about 32,000 acres. The Forest Service has no intention of extending any roads or truck trails into the primitive area and we trust that the same policy will continue to govern the area under state jurisdiction."[21] The application met with success in Washington D. C., and on April 21, 1931, the U. S. Forest Service created the San Jacinto Primitive Area.[22]

Throughout late 1930 and 1931, the various transactions were completed regarding the land swaps, and monies were raised for the necessary purchases. It took until 1933, thanks to delays in the Government Land Office paperwork, for the various entities to get actual title to the properties. It was at that point that improvements could begin to be made in the new Mt. San Jacinto State Park, as it was decided that the State Park would be improved first before it was officially opened. Because this occurred in the 1930s when various government agencies were attempting to put people to work, much of the work building trails and campgrounds to make the new park more accessible was accomplished by the Civilian Conservation Corp. From 1933 to 1936-37, various projects were undertaken to make the area a true state park. Mt. San Jacinto State Park was formally opened on June 19, 1937. Six days later, on June 25, 1937, the California State Park Commission unanimously adopted the policy of the National Forest Service in preservation of the San Jacinto Primitive Area. Therefore, by the summer of 1937, many people in the region and throughout Southern California were convinced that most of the San Jacinto Mountains had been set aside as wilderness area of some kind.

It was this setting into which the proposal for a desert-to-mountain aerial tramway was hurled, along with the ability to,

> . . . . acquire, construct or complete roads, highways, trams, tramways, aerial cableways, up-skis, ski-lifts, parking areas, skiing areas, areas for tobogganing, coasting, snowshoeing, sledding, ice skating, ski huts, hotels, pensions, lodges, restaurants, buses, buildings, and all other works, properties and structures necessary, convenient or useful for the development of winter sports, and any other recreational facilities within the territorial limits of the authority. [23]

But as we've seen, opposition to the tram came in the form of the powers of the proposed Mt. San Jacinto Winter Park Authority during the years of its creation. That was about to change, and change in a drastic way as many in the conservation community were to learn about Crocker's proposal.

Chapter 4 Endnotes

1. Robinson and Risher, 1993, p. 177; "How the United States Started Saving National Forests." www.wilderness.org, accessed January 17, 2023.
2. "Frequently Asked Questions" on the website of the U.S. Forest Service, https://www.fs.usda.gov/detail/sbnf/about-forest/?cid=FSBDEV7_007781, accessed February 5, 2023.
3. Hemet *News*, July 26, 1907.
4. Price, Overton (Associate U. S. Forester) to H. A. E. Marshall, April 20, 1908, in Robinson and Risher, 1993, p. 212.
5. Cree and his idea had several supporters, including the Riverside *Press*. At the time of Cree's proposal, the *Press* wrote that,

> The Palm canyon region is one of the most remarkable in the country and the groves of native palms are absolutely unique. Nothing like them is found anywhere else in the country and there are other features of the flora which are nearly as interesting. There is a wealth of cactus and the smoke tree and other remarkable desert plants and shrubs are found in abundance.
>
> Hardly of less interest is the San Jacinto peak and the trip from Strawberry Valley to the summit, by Hidden lake, is one of the most remarkable that can be taken in any mountain range in the country.
>
> The fact is not generally known, but it is possible to go from the Hemet lake valley down to the desert side directly into Palm canyon and thence to Palm Springs.
>
> Mr. Cree's idea is that if this park were created, a regular series of tourist excursions would be conducted. Parties could go by machine to Idyllwild and then by horseback to the summit of San Jacinto. Returning, they would take the autos to the Hemet dam and from there would go on horseback down to Palm canyon and the springs. From there a return trip by auto could be made to Riverside or the train could be taken at Palm Springs station.
>
> Taken leisurely, the trip need not be a hard one, and it could easily include a visit to the Soboba Indian reservation and the scenes made famous in Helen Hunt Jackson's "Ramona."

The Southern Pacific is already giving recognition to the importance of the Palm Springs section as a unique tourist resort by side-tracking excursions at the Palm Springs station and having parties taken to the springs and up Palm and Andreas Canyons.

The movement which Mr. Cree has started is a worthy and important one and deserves strong support. (Riverside *Daily Press*, February 8, 1917).

It can be seen here that Cree's idea was not completely one of preservation, but also of limited recreation through tourism between the mountains and the desert. Only a few years later, the idea of traveling from the mountains to the desert for tourism would manifest itself in the push to create a highway specifically for that purpose. That highway, the Pines-to-Palms Highway, ultimately did not go to Palm Springs but closer to Indio (see Lech, Steve – *For Tourism and a Good Night's Sleep: J. Win Wilson, Wilson Howell, and the Development of the Pines-to-Palms Highway*).

6. Robinson and Risher, 1993, p. 206. The primary difference between a National Park and National Monument is that National Parks are protected due to their scenic, inspirational, educational, and recreational value. National monuments have objects of historical, cultural, and/or scientific interest. Biggars, Ashley. "The Difference Between National Parks and Monuments." Available at www.outsidesonline.com, accessed January 18, 2023.
7. Hemet *News*, December 2, 1921.
8. Robinson and Risher, 1993, p. 208.
9. While constructing the railroad through Southern California in the 1870s, the Southern Pacific Company was given 20 square miles (or 12,800 acres) of land in alternating sections for each mile of track laid. This gave the Southern Pacific huge swaths of land in California. In Riverside County, much of the Coachella Valley and San Jacinto Mountains was handed over to the Southern Pacific as the subsidy for railroad construction (for more on the construction of the Southern Pacific Railroad through what would become Riverside County, see Lech, Steve – *Along the Old Roads*, Chapter 11).
10. Robinson and Risher, 1993, p. 208.
11. Proposals for a road were plentiful in the 1920s. In 1926, the Riverside County Board of Supervisors even asked for a preliminary survey for a possible route:

> Riverside county supervisors today authorized a reconnaissance by County Surveyor A. C. Fulmor for a route of the proposed road from Idyllwild to the San Jacinto peak, looking toward the ultimate building of that scenic highway. It was also decided to ask S. B. Show, head of the forest service, to send a surveyor to assist Mr. Fulmor in the preliminary survey, which would give approximate costs of the road as well as establishing a tentative route. Dr. C. Van Zwalenburg . . . . discussed the feasibility of the proposed road with the supervisors today. He stated that in his travels he was impressed with the desire of tourists to climb mountains – some of them much more inaccessible than the San Jacinto mountains. He is of the opinion that strong backing may be had for the project, which will make possible the construction of a scenic highway from Idyllwild to the peak, that would be comparable to the most beautiful mountain highways in other parts of the United States, and would offer a unique journey for automobile travelers and campers. (Riverside *Daily Press*, September 27, 1926).

12. Website of the Aldo Leopold Foundation (https://www.aldoleopold.org/about/aldo-leopold/), accessed February 5, 2021.
13. Leopold, Aldo, quoted in *The Sand County Almanac.*
14. Riverside *Press*, November 29, 1927. The Los Angeles group had already done their own study in the greater Riverside County area, proposing that Morongo Canyon, Thousand Palms Canyon, and Painted Canyon be added to a list of potential park sites in Southern California.
15. Riverside *Press*, January 30, 1928. This committee was made up of many members of various county clubs and agencies, including: Arthur C. Lovekin, Jonas Killian, J. Harrison Wright, Frank A. Miller, E. P. Clarke, John R. Gabbert, John E. Wherrel, Mrs. H. E. DeNyse, Samuel Cary Evans, R. H. Fuller, Howard Hays, Dr. W. W. Roblee, and Oscar Ford from Riverside; Frank L. Miller, C. D. Hamilton, Mrs. George L. Wing from Banning; Chester M. Kline, Ed Poorman, S. F. Sargent from San Jacinto; C. L. Emerson, R. H. Smith from Idyllwild; John E. King from Hemet; Mrs. Nellie Coffman from Palm Springs; Del R. Crane from Elsinore; W. F. Eldridge, James L. Davis and H. H. Burch from Corona; Walter Morgan from La Quinta; W. L. Percy from Beaumont; H. W. Postlethwaite from Coachella; August Rohrbacker from Nuevo;

T. Mahncke from Blythe; B. H. Hayes from Indio; Dr. H. J. Webber from the Citrus Experiment Station in Riverside; and Mrs. E. C. Talbot from Perris. In addition, all members of the Riverside County Board of Forestry were included – Joy. G. Jameson, French Gilman, Dr. J. B. Weston, E. B. Criddle, and A. E. Bottel. Also appointed to this committee was the full Board of Supervisors – T. C. Jameson, John Shaver, J. E. McGregor, T. F. Flaherty, and Harvey Johnson.

16. Approximately $91 million in 2021.
17. The concept of a state park for Mt. San Jacinto was clearly the most popular among residents in the region.
18. Hemet *News*, July 11, 1930.
19. Hemet *News*, July 18, 1930. These statements, and many others like them, will become important as the prospect of an aerial tramway gains momentum.
20. Gilligan, 1953, Vol. II, p. 1.
21. "History of Mt. San Jacinto State Park." https://www.msjnha.org/park-history, accessed January 24, 2023.
22. *Ibid*, p. 6.
23. California Legislature, S. B. 1051, 54th session (1941).

Chapter 5

The Opposition Begins

(The tramway proposal) permits exploitation of a primitive area through construction of hotels, eating places, etc., all privately owned; greatly exaggerates the suitability of the area for winter sports, and creates a business venture which will be free of state, county or local taxation.

Archie Twogood, President of the Riverside chapter of the Sierra Club, as quoted in the Riverside Daily Press, *March 16, 1945.*

A tour of California without a trip to the top of San Jacinto mountain would be as incomplete as would a trip to Colorado without a trip up Pike's Peak.

State Senator Nelson Dilworth, as quoted in The Desert Sun, *September 14, 1945.*

It was against the backdrop of efforts outlined in the previous chapter to preserve the San Jacinto Mountains that the idea of the aerial tramway and appurtenant winter sports facilities was proposed. In 1939, when the first surveys were started, the State Park was only two years old. By 1945, when the Mt. San Jacinto Winter Park Authority was created, the proposal of an aerial tramway leading from Palm Springs into the San Jacinto Mountains was ten years old. Countless discussions, demonstrations, meetings, and a herculean effort to get a financing authority approved through the California State Legislature had been accomplished to make the concept of the proposal a possibility.

Looking back roughly 75 years as we can today, given all of the environmental concerns and protections that we have in place today, we may wonder, then, why would a project such as the aerial tramway, plus appurtenant uses, not see a flurry of opposition to it? The proposal would not only cross areas within the Mt. San Jacinto State Park and National Forest areas, it would also open up those pristine areas to large-scale commercial winter sports development. In addition, constructing two large buildings (a valley station and mountain station) in environmentally-sensitive areas such as Chino Canyon and Long Valley, to say nothing of the grading, drilling, and blasting that would have to occur to secure the cable towers, would forever alter the landscape of that section of Mt. San Jacinto's northern escarpment.

The short answer to this question is that there was opposition, but it was not organized in any unified fashion. Prior to the 1930s and 1940s, there were really no true environmental "fights" like we know them today, pitting (usually) some entity wishing to develop an area against a unified group of environmental advocates hoping to maintain and preserve some of the original environment of a certain region. Environmental activism at the time of the aerial tramway proposal was generally centered around preserving areas for their uniqueness *before* any specific development was proposed, not in reaction to a development proposal. Therefore, the few voices that arose in opposition to creation of the Authority and the aerial tramway on the grounds of environmental concerns fell largely on indifferent ears.[1]

The first stated opposition to the tramway from an environmental perspective seems to have come from the Sierra Club's Riverside Chapter in April, 1941. This chapter, formed in 1932, had little to do with the creation of the wilderness areas in the San Jacinto Mountains, but opted to try to make a stand when the 1941 bills to create the Winter Park Authority were moving through the approval process. In essence, the Sierra Club passed a resolution directed at Governor Olsen requesting that he hold any approval of the bill pending a full investigation of the matter. The resolution stated, in part, that, "the bill appears to set up a private monopoly for the commercialization of public lands in the San Jacinto mountains, which would prevent general public access to the area, without payment of tolls."[2] This same opposition was mirrored in 1943.[3]

Despite the Sierra Club's lackluster push against the tram, 1943 was a pivotal year. It was at that time that noted conservationist and Indian enthusiast Harry Clebourne James began to direct his attention to the proposal, which began a nearly 20-year campaign to keep the Palm Springs Aerial Tramway merely a dream in the eyes of Francis Crocker.

Harry James was born in Ottawa, Toronto, Canada on April 25, 1896. He had come to California, specifically Los Angeles, in 1913, "admittedly moviestruck."[4]

The movie business did not work out, but after World War I, he began to involve himself with the outdoors, conservation issues, and

Harry James, 1940s (James San Jacinto Mountains Reserve).

teaching. In 1926, he and his soon-to-be wife Grace began the Trailfinders School for Boys in Altadena. This was a private school for junior-high aged boys wherein Grace James taught the basics and Harry (with others) taught about Indians, self-reliance, and other topics.

> That their school was successful could be attested by the nearly 40,000 boys that attended their full-time and part-time programs over the span of 40 years. Their formula for success was simple, incorporate the outdoors into all aspects of the curriculum, learn self-reliance and teamwork, and exercise the mind, body and spirit. The Trailfinder School took these junior high school-aged boys on outdoor expeditions that included retracing the travels of Lewis and Clark, and climbing summits in the Sierra Nevada, the Grand Tetons, and the Rocky Mountains. They spent summers on Hopi Reservations in Arizona learning Native American culture, as well as time in Europe to study the classics of music.[5]

With the Trailfinders and other groups he started, such as the Western Rangers, James had a built-in supply of eager people who held many of his beliefs about conservation. In 1923, James and some of his early Trailfinders began a movement to establish the San Gorgonio Wilderness in the San Bernardino Mountains. Mt. San Gorgonio, the tallest peak in Southern California, was ultimately conserved via a rather sneaky, yet productive manner. After his initial request to set aside the San Gorgonio Wilderness was turned down by U.S. Forest Service officials, James petitioned then-President Calvin Coolidge for the formation of Junipero Serra National Monument containing the same boundaries as his original proposal. Perhaps with Coolidge's approval, the U. S. Forest Service established the wilderness in 1925.[6]

Eighteen years later, James' school owned land in the San Jacinto Mountains, which was a regular retreat for them.[7] Counting on his previous success in the San Bernardino Mountains, as the proposal for the tramway was working its way through the legislative process, Harry James opted to use the same tactics he had used before. On June 7, 1943, he wrote a letter to President Franklin Delano Roosevelt asking that both San Gorgonio and San Jacinto Mountains be proclaimed as national monuments. (See Appendix C to read the letter outlining James' reasons for requesting national monument status).

Although this proposal was, in effect, a "Hail Mary" attempt at averting development in the two mountain regions, it had the effect of disturbing a hornet's nest. James was able to effect a letter-writing campaign in favor of his proposal by many of his Trailfinders members. However, that effort was met with severe opposition from many residents throughout the area, chambers of commerce, the State Park Commission, and others who believed that the current form of administration was adequate to protect the wilderness and did not need to be further bogged down. The National Park Service even went so far as to ask various entities their thoughts, and concluded that "the Forest Service and State officials are quite anxious to maintain the 'wilderness character' of the mountain."[8]

Once the dust had settled regarding Harry James' proposal, things would not be the same regarding the tramway project. As Richard Davis pointed out,

> . . . James's proposal had some positive effects. For the first time criticism of the tramway based on wilderness purist grounds had been forced into public notice. Conservationist organizations were reminded that there were indeed friends of wilderness in Southern California. The Forest Service was finally confronted with evidence of public concern for the maintenance of the San Jacinto Primitive Area.[9]

To that might be added the fact that Harry James had become committed to defeating the proposed Palm Springs Tramway, and keeping the San Jacinto Wilderness Area as he perceived it was to be.

With the effective end of a proposal to create a National Park out of Mt. San Jacinto, James nonetheless pledged to continue fighting the proposed tramway. On September 8, 1944, he addressed an audience in Banning and stated that "he would continue to fight the Tramway. His organization is opposing the Mt. San Jacinto tramway on the theory that the area comprising Mt. San Jacinto State Park should remain a primitive area for the sole use of hikers and horseback riders."[10]

Postcard view of Mt. San Gorgonio by Stephen Willard, 1935 (Author's collection).

Throughout the summer and fall of 1944, James worked behind the scenes to engender support for his cause. With the prospect of the tramway and other uses invading the State Park area just a few years after the park's creation, James was able to secure more support. Leading up to the State Park Commission meeting at the Desert Inn in Palm Springs on January 4, 1945, James had added the support of the Federation of Western Outdoor Clubs and also the Sierra Club.

When the Park Commission meeting was held, Francis Crocker, who was called upon to give an overview of the project, appears to have gone slightly on the defensive in delivering his speech. While extolling the virtues of the tramway, Crocker explained that,

> it was the desire of the [tramway] committee to obtain legislation which would make the construction of the aerial tramway a post-war project which would not be paid for by the taxpayers of the State but would be paid for by the passengers of the tramway . . . . . It was pointed out at the hearing that the Palm Springs sponsors of the bill are not interested in securing any rights or concessions in the State Park, nor are they interested in making profits from the tramway itself. Their principal objective is to provide a means of access into a winter sports area which is now entirely inaccessible from the eastern side of Mt. San Jacinto.[11]

Several members of the Park Commission privately endorsed the tramway plan, although the Commission did not take a position on it.

As we saw in Chapter 3, the bill creating the Mt. San Jacinto Winter Park Authority was signed into law on June 25, 1945. By this time, several entities both inside and outside of Riverside County had been convinced of the viability and necessity of having a spectacular aerial tramway whisking people to the heights of Mt. San Jacinto within just a few minutes. On the other hand, the opposition to the bill had been somewhat disjointed, resulting in only moderate support.

Despite their defeat, the opposition continued to press forward in the hopes that the construction of the tramway and other uses could be defeated. One method they used, rightfully or otherwise, was to blame the passage of the Winter Park Authority bill on sneakiness – accomplishing it while many people were away or otherwise preoccupied with war-time duties. As we have seen, though, the efforts to secure approval of the bill started before the war, and perseverance won out on the part of the proponents. The State legislature only met during the first months of odd-numbered years, so opponents had few opportunities to plead their case. Still, Joe Momyer, an ardent opposition member, would write later,

> Our greatest stumbling block ever since the passage of the Mt. San Jacinto Winter Park Act by the Legislature in 1945, *when most of us were in war work or service*, [emphasis added] has been the impression that the Act represented a mandate from the people of California . . . .[12]

Regardless of any deviousness on the part of the tramway proponents, opposition to the tramway was mounting among outdoor groups and what we today may call environmental groups. In March, 1945, Francis Crocker and Earl Coffman sat down with representatives of the Sierra Club in Riverside to address their concerns. Instead, the leaders of the opposition went on record as stating that the tramway would,

> Permit exploitation of a primitive area through construction of hotels, eating places, etc., all privately owned; [the tramway bill] greatly exaggerates the suitability of the area for winter sports, and creates a business venture which will be free of state, county or local taxation.

In addition, the Riverside *Press* went on to say that, "The hiking club officials declare that the winter sports season at the top of the tram lift would be short; skiing slopes are scarce, and the best of them are dangerous. . . . . A growing commercialism is feared in this area and in other state parks if the tramway bill is passed."[13]

Although the few opponents of the tramway were not successful in their early attempts, one thing that did work in their favor was a slowly-galvanizing cadre of people from many of those early outdoor/environmental groups towards defeating the tramway effort. With the passage of the Winter Park Authority legislation, the end of the war, and the return to civilian life for many, efforts to try to derail the project could now be given the needed time and effort. No one knew this more than Harry James, and he used the immediate post-war period to garner further support and make his position known.

Chapter 5 Endnotes

1. The reader should keep in mind that there was opposition to the bills early on, but from the standpoint of the powers proposed to be granted to the Winter Park Authority, NOT on environmental or conservation grounds.
2. Riverside *Daily Press*, April 29, 1941.
3. Davis, August 1973, pp. 213-214.
4. Jennings, 1979, p. 6.
5. "Trailfinders History."
6. Jennings, 1979, p. 6.
7. Harry James and his wife Grace also built a cabin they called Lolomi Lodge on the property. Today, this is the James San Jacinto Mountains Reserve of the University of California's Natural Reserve System.
8. Davis, August 1973, p. 218.
9. *Ibid*, p. 219.
10. *The Desert Sun*, September 15, 1944.
11. *The Desert Sun,* January 5, 1945.
12. Momyer, January, 1955, p. 18.
13. Riverside *Daily Press*, March 16, 1945.

Lolomi Lodge, the mountain home of Harry and Grace James (James San Jacinto Mountains Reserve).

Chapter 6

Work Gets Underway

I don't know of anything which can be of greater publicity value to this area as well as to the entire state than the Mt. San Jacinto Aerial Tramway. It is a project which grips the imagination.

Joseph R. Knowland, president of the California State Parks Commission, as quoted in the Palm Springs Limelight, *March 7, 1946*

We need to think in terms of permanent recreational values for the people who live in Southern California rather than in terms of added superficial attractions to bring a greater flood of transient tourists through the state.

Joe Momyer, as quoted in "Wilderness Recreation for a Metropolitan Area," September, 1949

Naturally, the signing of the enabling legislation into law by Governor Earl Warren was a cause for celebration in Palm Springs. Robert Ransom, President of the Palm Springs Chamber of Commerce, did not hold back his enthusiasm:

> There will be nothing else like it in the world . . . . it will open to the general public one of the most beautiful mountain areas of the West heretofore accessible only by hiking or horseback. Particularly famous will be the winter sports to which the tramway will be the gateway during the winter months. The snows of the upper altitudes of the San Jacinto mountains are rated as among the finest in California for skiing. And it is obvious that the summer time travel to the cool, high sections of the San Jacintos will be tremendous.[1]

On July 23, 1945, Ransom also presided over a "victory" dinner held at the Mission Inn.[2] Boosters from all over Southern California attended. That next weekend, July 28-29, a "victory ride" was undertaken by 70 people from Idyllwild to San Jacinto Peak. Earl Coffman and Frances Crocker were in attendance, as were many representatives of various chambers of commerce. At the campfire dinner, Palm Springs Assemblyman Philip Boyd explained some of the legislative hurdles that were encountered and overcome in the approval process. Earl Coffman gave details about the proposed tramway, and then went on to discuss what he had recently traveled across country to inspect – the Cannon Mountain Aerial Passenger Tramway in Franconia Notch, New Hampshire.[3]

Cannon Mountain Aerial Passenger Tramway

The Cannon Mountain Aerial Passenger Tramway was the first of its kind in the United States, and had a tremendous impact on the proponents of the proposed Mt. San Jacinto Tramway. In the early 1930s, people began to see the potential for skiing on Cannon Mountain in the White Mountains area of northern New Hampshire. Cannon Mountain lay in the Franconia Notch State Park, which was visited often by a renowned American skier by the name of Alexander Bright. While skiing in Europe, Bright had seen the use of cable tramways for ski lifts, and thought the Cannon Mountain area would suit such a tramway. Over the next few years, promoters appealed to the New Hampshire State Legislature for approval and, once received, appealed again for funding. The end result was the opening of the Cannon Mountain Aerial Passenger Tramway on June 28, 1938, just in time to be able to show off the new facility and work out any issues prior to the 1938-1939 ski season.

But it wasn't just skiing that prompted the construction of the Cannon Mountain Tramway. Situated in the famous White Mountains and overlooked by the famous Old Man of the Mountain, the Franconia Notch State Park was a haven for sightseers and nature-lovers too.

(Above) Cover of souvenir booklet for the Cannon Mountain Tram

(Right) Postcard view of the Cannon Mountain Aerial Tramway, 1939 (Author's collection)

New Hampshire's "Old Man of the Mountain"
as seen prior to its collapse on May 3, 2003 (Internet photo).

> For well over a hundred years New Hampshire has loved The Old Man of the Mountains, and each year thousands of visitors come to stand in wonder . . . . . and now just half a mile north the State has completed the first aerial passenger tramway in North America, by means of which twenty-seven people can make a thrilling aerial ascent of 2,022 feet in five minutes and twenty-eight seconds, with all northern New England spread out before them.[4]

The Cannon Mountain Tramway had many aspects that were proposed for the San Jacinto Mountain one, including rectangular cars with lots of glass and no seats, a "Valley Station" and a "Mountain Station," and appeal to skiers from a large area. The Cannon Mountain route had been selected due to the fact that it was already a major tourist route and required only a minimum of forest cutting, thereby reducing environmental impacts from the tramway.[5]

By the time the Mt. San Jacinto Aerial Tramway had been approved and work had begun on it, the Cannon Mountain Tramway had been in operation for around 10 years. It had been a popular facility and had managed to be profitable. Therefore, it was brought up many times as an example of a successful tramway project that was popular, functional, and economically viable. Proponents would refer to the project many times during the ensuing years.

NEXT STEPS

The next steps in the construction of the tramway were already being contemplated at the July 23 dinner at the Mission Inn. There, Robert Ransom of the Palm Springs Chamber indicated that work should begin immediately on choosing the people from Palm Springs and Riverside County who would make up 4/7 of the Mt. San Jacinto Winter Park Authority board. At the dinner, a committee was appointed to begin screening people for the two appointees from Riverside County.[6]

On September 19, 1945, the first two members of the Authority board were named – Palm Springs' Earl Coffman and John R. E. Chaffey. Interestingly, Francis Crocker was not named to the board, citing "he felt he did not have the time to do justice to the very important task."[7] Two weeks later, the Riverside County Board of Supervisors named V. W. Grubbs, a flooring contractor from Riverside, and J. G. Nussbaum of Idyllwild to the Authority's board, rounding out the local appointees. A few weeks after that, Governor Earl Warren appointed Harrold English, a prominent engineer from Los Angeles and part-time Palm Springs resident, Leonard Firestone of the Firestone Tire and Rubber Company, and John McKenzie of Inglewood, who was the manager of the Hollywood Park race track, to the board, completing the seven members stipulated under the legislation.[8] At the new board's first meeting, held on November 24 at the Desert Inn in Palm Springs, Earl Coffman was elected president of the board and John R. E. Chaffey became secretary.[9]

After the holidays, the Winter Park Authority Board wasted no time getting to work. During the war, the original consulting firm of Modjeski and Masters had concentrated on war work and the ties that they had with the Palm Springs people had been severed. Therefore, by the end of January, 1946, the Authority had two new engineering and equipment firms in town looking at the plans for the tramway and offering advice while going through what we today might call a Request for Proposals process. The first of these firms was the Interstate

Equipment Company of Elizabeth, New Jersey. This firm specialized in municipal construction, industrial equipment, and the appurtenant supplies. Interstate Equipment had installed hundreds of cableways throughout the world, mostly for materials transportation, but had done some passenger work in Europe. The other one was the American Steel and Wire Company of New Haven, Connecticut. Representing American Steel was Gordon E. Bannerman and Roland Peabody, both of whom had been instrumental in the design and construction of the Cannon Mountain Aerial Tramway in Franconia Notch, New Hampshire.

In addition to the engineering firms, there was George Warfield of the firm of Coverdale and Colepitts of New York. This was a transportation engineering firm specializing in large-scale transportation infrastructure. Warfield's assignment was to complete a new survey of the tramway route and also an economic feasibility study of the project. Unfortunately for the Winter Park Authority, their plan to use some Federal Reconstruction Finance Corporation funds which had become available to jurisdictions after the war to stimulate construction had already been allocated to other projects. So, the Winter Park Authority had to go to residents and businesses in Palm Springs, hat in hand, to raise enough capital to pay for the various studies.[10]

After ten days of intense study on the part of Bannerman and Peabody, both men made statements to the effect that the tramway could work and would be economically feasible. Roland Peabody, the managing director of the Cannon Mountain Aerial Tramway, was the more optimistic of the two;

> From the studies made of the contour maps and aerial views, the mountain above 8500 feet lends itself to outstanding recreational developments for both summer and winter use. Slopes appear to be of proper grades to make them ideal for the average skier, which is the majority of the tramway winter business from our experience at Cannon Mountain in Franconia, New Hampshire. With ample transportation capacity from the highway to the valley station of the tramway contemplated here, the project should be a financial success.[11]

Gordon Bannerman surveys the desert from the location of the future Mountain Station, 1950. This picture was featured in the special edition of the Palm Springs Villager that was published in anticipation of the construction of the Tramway in 1950 (Palm Springs Life archive).

On February 24, 1946, the first of the proposals for tramway construction was submitted. The proposal by Interstate Equipment was given to the Authority Board. It was held pending at least one other, and possibly two. On April 27, the Board heard from Gordon Bannerman of American Steel and Wire. It seems from the outset that this proposal was the anticipated one. Because of the length of the tramway, the proposal called for three stations – a Chino Canyon station, an intermediate station, and a mountain station. Passengers would get on at the lower station, ride to the mid-point, get off, and board another car for the mountain station. The cars would hold 54 passengers, which would be exactly twice the number in the cars at Franconia Notch. Bannerman indicated that if his company were to get the contract by the summer, he was confident that the first passengers would be riding the tramway in the fall of 1947.[12]

The end of May brought news that the Mt. San Jacinto Winter Park Authority had made a unanimous decision to award the contract to the American Steel and Wire Company under Gordon Bannerman. Bannerman was quick to mention, however, that his company would be doing the engineering and survey work only – the actual construction would be accomplished by two sub-contractors, the Consolidated Steel and Wire Company of Los Angeles, which would furnish and construct the towers and cabling, and the Morrison-Knudson Company of Boise, Idaho, which would do the footings, roads, parking areas, and buildings. Morrison-Knudson had been a co-contractor on the Hoover Dam, so they were not unknown in tackling large projects.[13] In fact, they already had survey crews in Chino Canyon when the news was announced.

Unfortunately for the proponents of the project, post-war realities began to set in by the end of 1946. Labor and material shortages forced the Authority board to put the project on hold, at least for a few months. In a statement to the press, President Earl Coffman indicated that,

> It was the opinion of the members that actual construction be deferred until equipment, labor and materials, now being used for necessary construction become available for recreational projects such as the tramway. The authority believes this situation may be cleared up within the next six or eight months and hope at that time that construction can begin.[14]

It wasn't only material and labor shortages that were hindering construction of the tramway. Despite all of the engineers on the ground performing various surveys and completing studies, no one could or would propose a concrete cost to construct the facilities. Several times, Earl Coffman was quoted as being frustrated with this factor. The volatility of markets at the time made establishing a true cost very difficult. By the beginning of 1947, though, one thing was becoming obvious – the tramway would cost more than the $3,000,000 that the Mt. San Jacinto Winter Park Authority was authorized to bond for by the 1945 legislation. That legislation, the culmination of three attempts to create the Authority, had used the engineering surveys and cost estimates done by Modjeski and Masters *before* the war. Postwar realities and markets made for construction and materials costs that were two to three times more, according to Coffman.[15] Regardless, the Authority was only allowed to bond for no more than $3,000,000.

In order to correct this issue, the Authority appealed to State Assemblyman Philip Boyd, who was a staunch supporter of the tram. In meetings with him, they opted to introduce new legislation that would give the Authority another $1,000,000 in bonding capability so that they could begin construction. Throughout the spring of 1947, Boyd's bill, with amendments, made its way through the legislative process. A major change occurred when the bond restriction was lifted, in effect giving the Authority carte blanche to bond for as much as they needed to finance construction. In the end, this bill passed, and was signed into law by Governor Warren on April 23, 1947.[16]

With the removal of a fixed bonding amount, seemingly, construction could begin. Gordon Bannerman was enthusiastic about saying that once construction began, it would take about 20 months to complete.[17] By early summer, Earl Coffman was predicting a date of late summer to begin construction, but by August, it looked like material shortages may postpone construction a little while longer.[18] By September, though, this had not happened. The final cost of the project was still up in the air. Because of this, the Authority could not begin selling bonds, and therefore money could not be raised, and construction could not start.[19]

This impasse continued through the fall of 1947. During that time, it was announced that the three major firms involved so far, American Steel and Wire, Consolidated Steel, and Morrison-Knudson, would work as one in constructing the tramway. While that did help to keep news of the tramway in the spotlight, it appears to have changed little towards hastening construction, which by the fall of 1947 was now slated to begin during the summer of 1948.[20]

As winter approached, and snow began to fall on Mt. San Jacinto, surveyors of the Morrison-Knudson firm began to do surveys and boring tests on their own accord, hoping to hasten construction once the money was in hand. It was a good thing they did, because the hiatus in construction, and even news about when construction would start, continued well into 1948. On May 18 of that year, the *Desert Sun* tried to explain the entire situation to its readers:

> The most frequent question asked the Desert Sun is: "When will the Tramway be built?" The answer still is: We don't know. Apparently neither does the Mt. San Jacinto Winter Park Authority. . . . . It is quite apparent . . . . that it was

1948 advertising view of the proposed Palm Springs Aerial Tramway with features listed. Note the 2-stage alignment of the tramway, necessitating a stop in the middle of the route (Palm Springs Life archive).

> INTENDED construction be started a year ago last March. Note that [the 1947 legislation removing the bond restrictions] says that engineering studies are complete, estimates have been made by responsible contractors who are available to bid and undertake construction. Now, 14 months later, we are advised that borings are being made at tower sites to determine the probable cost of erecting such towers. The Authority tells us that responsible companies will not bid on the job because: 1) They do not have sufficient engineering data on which to base their bid. 2) The labor market is too unstable to undertake a job of this size at a fixed bid. In the meantime, the "favorable market conditions" for the sale of the bonds has long since passed, and the "approaching off-season months" have come and gone a couple of times. As a result, the "public peace, health and safety" of the people of the State of California have not been "preserved." We're not losing sleep over the public peace, health and safety, however; it's the failure of the Tramway Authority to get the project under way that causes our people to wonder and worry.[21]

It took until the beginning of August, 1948, but finally the go-ahead was given to do exploratory work on the foundations of the tram's towers. Funds for these tests were subscribed by private donations to at least get the project moving to a certain degree. This seems to have been the holdup so far as getting the needed information to fix a final bid price for the overall construction.[22] At that time, it was assumed that testing would begin in September.[23]

Luckily for the Authority, this time work actually did begin. Around September 15, groups of engineers packed their way into Chino Canyon and began doing some of the necessary work to establish where the stations and towers would go. After five days in the field, George Bannerman announced that not only would there be the three stations – in Chino Canyon, in Long Valley, and halfway up the slope, but there would need to be a total of six towers to direct the cables upon which the tramway would ride. Soon, the groups who were already on the ground were joined by two more men, Elmer Lloyd, the Chief Tramway Engineer, and Ellis Dahlgren, Construction Engineer. With actual work commencing, formal offices were rented in Palm Springs at 460 North Palm Canyon Drive.[24] It was estimated at that time that the resurveying work and sub-surface site analysis would take about six months.[25]

Meanwhile, as the engineers were at work on the mountain side, Earl Coffman and others were consulting with Tommy Tyndall as to the ski opportunities afforded from the proposed tramway terminus. Tyndall, a powerhouse for recreational skiing in Southern California in the 1940s and 1950s, was called upon to give his expertise on where ski facilities should be placed and how additional lifts could transport visitors from the tramway's upper station.

With 1948 coming to a close, Authority members and Palm Springs residents alike eagerly waited for the results of the newest survey and engineering report, which most anticipated would be finished sometime in January, 1949. By the end of the year, Francis Crocker, considered to be the "Father" of the tramway, had joined the Winter Park Authority Board, having taken the place of John Chaffey who resigned.

Chapter 6 Endnotes

1. Riverside *Daily Press*, June 27, 1945.
2. Riverside *Daily Press*, July 23, 1945.
3. Riverside *Daily Press*, July 30, 1945.
4. *America's First Aerial Tramway*, 1938, pp. 2-3.
5. https://www.cannonmt.com/mountain/cannon-history, accessed December 10, 2021.
6. *The Desert Sun*, August 10, 1945. As an aside, it was mentioned in the article that both Riverside County Supervisors Robert Dillan and Walter Pittman attended the dinner, and agreed that the appointment of a committee to screen applicants was a good idea, and that they would "welcome such recommendations after careful study." This was clearly done in the years prior to California's enacting the Brown Act, which mandates that all public decisions be made in public meetings with public input, and that the public be notified of public hearings.
7. *The Desert Sun*, September 21, 1945.
8. *The Desert Sun*, September 21, 1945, October 5, 1945, and November 16, 1945.
9. *The Desert Sun*, November 30, 1945.
10. *The Desert Sun*, January 25, 1946.
11. *The Desert Sun*, February 8, 1946.
12. *The Desert Sun*, April 26, 1946.
13. *The Desert Sun*, May 31, 1946.
14. *The Desert Sun*, December 10, 1946.
15. *The Desert Sun*, February 11, 1947.
16. Palm Springs *Limelight*, April 24, 1947.
17. *The Desert Sun*, April 25, 1947.
18. *The Desert Sun*, June 24 and August 5, 1947
19. *The Desert Sun*, September 9, 1947.
20. *The Desert Sun*, November 11, 1947.
21. *The Desert Sun*, May 18, 1948.
22. Palm Springs *Limelight*, August 6, 1948.
23. *The Desert Sun*, August 20, 1948.
24. Palm Springs *Limelight*, September 28, 1948.
25. *The Desert Sun*, October 12, 1948.

Chapter 7

Opposition Mounts

Could it be that the sponsors of the project have more up their sleeves than a multimillion-dollar tramway into a poor ski area for winter sports enthusiasts? Could it be that this invasion of a wilderness area is the "foot in the door" approach to the ultimate building of a Palm Springs "summer resort"?

Edward C. Suydam, Pasadena resident,
Los Angeles Times *Letters to the Editor, May 23, 1949*

The Tramway seems to be about a year away but it is definitely in prospect.

Oliver Janes, as quoted in The Desert Sun, *January 30, 1948.*

The delays of 1947 and 1948 did more than simply postpone the dreams of Crocker, Coffman, and the many other proponents of the tramway. They also gave time to opponents of the project to garner more support for their cause. It was during this time that Harry James and his growing cadre of tramway opponents made their voices and arguments heard to whomever would listen, and enlist the help and guidance of more people who were coming around to the idea of holding the State of California and the National Forest Service to their promises, true or otherwise, of protecting the Mt. San Jacinto Wilderness Area and maintaining it in a wilderness condition.

During the 1946 – 1948 era, little could be done to effect change in the proposal, or the outright denial of it. As seen in the previous chapter, most of this time was spent conducting surveys, hiring engineering firms, and of course, waiting while cost estimates and funding were in flux. However, while much of the surveys, negotiations, and brokering of deals necessarily occurred out of the public's eye, the opposition had one major opportunity to make their case, and that was during the hearings on adoption of an agreement between the Winter Park Authority and the State Park Commission. As stipulated in the enabling legislation, an agreement between the parties was mandatory in order for construction to occur within the boundaries of the State Park. Therefore, opponents of the tramway project set their sights on that agreement, and the meeting of the State Parks Commission at which the agreement would be heard.

In reviewing the enabling legislation, opponents of the project saw an opportunity to overturn the project at the State Park Commission level. While the legislation granted the ability to construct all means of winter sports facilities, it did so with the proviso that, "any of the powers granted herein shall be exercised within the territorial limits of Mount San Jacinto State Park only by the *express consent and under contract with the State Park Commission*."[1] (emphasis added). The opportunity the opposition saw was simple – get the State Park Commission to deny the agreement, and the project could not be constructed.

This line of thinking, though, was not that assured. The State Park Commission had been sold on the tramway project back in early 1945, just a few months before the legislation was enacted. In addition, the President of the Commission, Joseph Knowland, was a frequent visitor to Palm Springs and an ardent supporter of the project: "I don't know of anything which can be of greater publicity value to this area as well as to the entire state than the Mt. San Jacinto Aerial Tramway. It is a project which grips the imagination" he told the Palm Springs *Limelight*.[2]

The hearing for the agreement between the Authority and the State Park Commission was held in Los Angeles on December 17, 1948. At that time, proponents requested approval of an agreement which would allow construction of the proposed tramway over State Park property, plus the construction of the terminal facility in Long Valley (i.e. the upper or Mountain Station). At this meeting, the opposition delegation was sizable. Representatives from the Sierra Club, the Federation of Western Outdoor Clubs, the National Parks Association, and many others took their turns arguing that approval of the agreement would in effect be a violation of policies previously adopted by former State Parks Commissions which, it was argued, "dedicated the entire Mount San Jacinto area, both federal and state lands, as a wilderness free from artificial means of access."[3]

Unfortunately for the opposition, the Commission saw things in a totally different way. They apparently did not address the wilderness issue. Instead, they approved the agreement arguing that the original legislation's intent was to give a mandate to the State to approve an agreement. In other words, the language stating, "any of the powers

"Entrance to Strawberry Valley" postcard, c. 1915 (Author's collection).

granted herein shall be exercised . . . only by the express consent and under contract with the State Park Commission" in effect told the Commission that the legislature had approved the project, and their approval was effectively a mandate for the State Parks Commission to enter into an agreement with the proponents to construct the tramway. In the view of the Commission, approving an agreement was not up for debate as the opponents had hoped.

With this defeat, once again, Harry James resorted to the "Hail Mary" tactic. He circulated a petition for signatures from several members of various outdoor groups, including the Sierra Club, Izaak Walton League, Audubon Society, and the Southern California Outdoor Federation, asking that the State Legislature simply repeal the 1945 Winter Park Authority Act. With enough signatures, James was able to find one Assemblyman – Vernon Kilpatrick of Los Angeles – to sponsor the bill. In January, 1949, the California Legislature began its hearing, and on the 24th of that month, Kilpatrick introduced AB 1337, "An act to repeal the Mount San Jacinto Winter Park Authority Act, Chapter 1040 of the Statutes of 1945, relating to the creation, powers, and duties of the Mount San Jacinto Winter Park Authority."[4]

This move incensed many pro-tramway activists, who immediately editorialized in the Palm Springs *Limelight News* that,

> Several "conservation" groups this week demanded repeal of the State act sponsoring construction of the proposed Tramway . . . . . These "conservationists" claimed the Tramway would establish a precedent for breaking into an area of a National Forest . . . . . Most of the area that will be made accessible by the erection of the Tram is now so desolate that probably less than a score of fishermen, hunters and hikers . . . . entered the region in the past year. Primitive scenery is a beautiful thing, but why should the beauty be forever reserved for a select few? The road built into Yosemite National Park doesn't spoil the primitive beauty of that natural paradise. . . . by observing sensible restrictions and regulations, surely San Jacinto's primitive beauty would remain as well conserved as that of Yosemite.[5]

Within a few weeks, it was becoming obvious that any support for simply overturning the 1945 Act was deteriorating. Many in the Legislature and throughout Southern California knew that much effort and time had been put into the Act, not to mention all of the work and studies done by the Authority. Most saw the actions of Harry James and his cohorts as "too little, too late" and that they should have been involved earlier if they truly had wanted to stop the Tramway. By the beginning of February, Assemblyman Kilpatrick is quoted as saying that he had introduced AB 1337 as a courtesy to James and the others who had signed the petition, but that he was not going to press the issue further.[6] AB 1337 died without a hearing of the full Assembly.[7]

The defeat of AB 1337 marked the second time the opponents had tried unsuccessfully to keep the tramway from being built. Unlike most instances in which something like this happens, the dual defeats had the effect of galvanizing and expanding the opposition. One advantage the opposition had now was an increased understanding of their position, and the ability to get their position heard by many more people. Knowing that opposing the Tramway at the local level would get them nowhere, they began to turn their attention to opposing the project at the State and Federal level. Now, too, their arguments had coalesced into tangible positions that would be stated time and again in various outdoor-related publications, and anywhere else they could be heard. Before we move on with the next steps in the fight against the Tramway, it would be a good idea to take an in-depth look at the arguments put forth by the opposition.

Arguments Against the Tramway

By about 1950, four main points had coalesced into the heart of the opposition to the Mt. San Jacinto Winter Park Authority's proposed tramway. The opposition at this time had two main standard bearers - Harry James, the original leader of the opposition, and Guy Fleming, who, in retirement, was now poised to become the number two man in the opposition. In separate ways, they sought to outline the arguments to a wider audience. Between 1948 and 1950, both men penned articles in various publications devoted to conservation interests. James' "The San Jacinto Winter Park Summer Resort Scheme," published in *The Living Wilderness*, a quarterly magazine publication put out by the Wilderness Society, sought to bring nationwide attention to the effort.[8] Similarly, Guy Fleming published "Shall We Cherish and Maintain the San Jacinto Wild Area?" in the Sierra Club Bulletin, and "The Mount San Jacinto Tramway Scheme" in the National Parks Magazine.

Argument 1

Construction of the Tramway Would Set a Precedent for Encroaching into a Primitive Area of a National Forest and State Park and Thereby Endanger Other Similar Places

In this argument, many dwelled upon the uniqueness of Mt. San Jacinto and the fact that much of the area remained unspoiled. Describing the area in general, James for one states that Mt. San Jacinto's, "northeast escarpment, rising in spectacular castellated cliffs from the low Colorado Desert at around 400 feet above sea level to alpine crests well above the 10,000-foot elevation, makes it a truly dramatic mountain mass. On its southwestern slopes there are magnificent coniferous forests and lush mountain meadows, many of which are waist-high with fern and azalea. Flowering dogwood borders many of the fine mountains streams."[9]

Scientifically speaking, Mt. San Jacinto is an area where several life zones come together. These life zones are never found so close together as there are at Mt. San Jacinto, and in many instances, they are almost interlaced. From 1896 to 1901, an extensive botanical survey was conducted of the San Jacinto Mountains by Dr. Harvey Monroe Hall of the University of California. One of his many conclusions was that,

View down Snow Creek from San Jacinto Peak c. 1920 (Author's collection).

Postcard view of Mt. San Jacinto by Stephen Willard, 1944 (Author's collection).

> We thus have the six zones very much crowded together, and the upper four almost in superposition. There is probably no place in North America where the alpine and Sonoran floras are in such proximity as they are on San Jacinto Mountain.[10]

Not only is this area known for unique vistas and its closely-packed life zone features, but this region is very accessible from throughout Southern California. Joe Momyer, a San Bernardino resident who at the time was the President of the Riverside Chapter of the Sierra Club, stated that this "beautiful and unspoiled mountain wilderness into which one may hike or ride horseback and enjoy alpine scenery and environment . . . . is within four hours of downtown Los Angeles by car and on foot . . . . The mountains are ideally situated in the center of the six southern counties . . . . ."[11]

Building on this aspect of the argument, it was then pointed out that the effort to preserve the San Jacinto Mountains was not a new one. For nearly 50 years, people had seen the wilderness potential of the region. Starting with the 1893 establishment of the San Bernardino National Forest that included the San Jacinto Mountains, through the 1931 formation of the San Jacinto Primitive Area, then the 1933 establishment of Mt. San Jacinto State Park, efforts at preserving the San Jacinto Mountains in a wilderness state had been many. Several instances were offered to demonstrate that the intent of those who worked on the aforementioned efforts did so with the understanding that the area would be left in some sort of wilderness state. "The preservation of the area now is in large measure dependent on an understanding of the history of its dedication by the public to such preservation, and the understanding that the state and federal agencies responsible to the public for these lands were in agreement on this dedication."[12]

Similarly, Guy Fleming, in his essay "Shall We Cherish and Maintain the San Jacinto Wild Area?" reminds his readers that none other than Frederick Law Olmstead developed his own "Statement in Regard to the Region Culminating in the San Jacinto Mountains," which was adopted by the California State Parks Commission at its meeting of March 25, 1929. In it, Olmstead talks of,

> creating . . . a consolidated body of continuous national forest land, definitely withdrawn as a "wilderness area," in which any lumbering operations or building operations or road construction shall be permanently prohibited and which shall be administered for public recreation of kinds suitable for a wilderness by the Forest Service, with close cooperation between the state park service and the national forest Service in trail building, protection, and policing on both areas considered as one functional unit.[13]

A further citation came from Newton Drury, the state park acquisition officer in the 1930s, who had submitted a 1937 memo to Joseph R. Knowland, at the time the chair of the State Park Commission, on the subject of the potential for an automobile road to the summit of Mt. San Jacinto. Knowland's reply was to state that,

> when Mt. San Jacinto State park was established in 1933, while there was no formal action by the State Park Commission, a tacit understanding was reached with the U. S. Forest Service and the proponents of the project that the entire park area of approximately 12,700 acres would be administrated as a "primitive region," to be penetrated only by foot and horse trails. There has been no plan for an automobile road to the summit.[14]

Finally, James reiterates the words of Guy Fleming to sum up the position of this argument succinctly:

> If it is the will and desire of the People of California to retain Mount San Jacinto State Park as a wilderness area, and be assured that its primitive aspects will be held in perpetuity they must be aggressive in pressing their case upon the grounds that the State Legislature in creating the Mount San Jacinto Winter Park Authority violated a definite and publicly expressed agreement made in good faith between the State Park Commission, representing the people of California, and the United States forest Service, representing the people of this nation, that Mount San Jacinto be a definite part of the federally dedicated San Jacinto Wild Area and subject to the policies accepted for the protection and maintenance of established wilderness areas.[15]

Keeping the above points in mind, namely the uniqueness of San Jacinto plus the previous efforts to maintain it in a wilderness state, James, Fleming, and many others argued that approving and constructing a cable tramway and accompanying winter sports venues would set a very dangerous precedent – one that could be used to allow similar large-scale sports and/or recreation developments to be constructed in other unique wilderness areas.

Ernie Maxwell Trail, San Jacinto Mountains (Author's photo).

Argument 2

The Mt. San Jacinto Winter Park Authority Enabling Act was Passed Solely for the Benefit of Palm Springs and is Too Broad with Respect to What the Authority May Do

The argument here is quite simple – the Mt. San Jacinto Winter Park Authority was created solely as a legal instrument of the promoters of Palm Springs who were seeking to exploit the San Jacinto Mountains for their own purposes. The Authority was established by legislative actions taken during the war, and was created "in war time circumstances and under conditions which California conservationists have deeply resented."[16]

James recounts how the original plan was to call the Authority the Palm Springs Winter Park Authority, and give this entity nearly total control of lands that had previously been placed under the auspices of both the State of California and the U. S. National Forest Service.[17] The bills stressed the unique opportunities for winter sports in the San Jacinto Mountains, just minutes away from Palm Springs. Although some small protests were made, the attempts to pass the bill were continuous. In 1945, it was finally passed and enacted by the Governor.

> It was war time. Many defenders of the San Jacinto wilderness were in distant lands. Others were distracted by war requirements at home. Protests were made, it is true (even from as far away as Burma), but it was not possible to activate the really dynamic campaign against the measure which the event proved was necessary.[18]

Not only was the enabling legislation drafted and approved during wartime, it was argued, the legislation gave the Authority immense powers:

> Amazing concessions were made. The act provides, for example, that "the Authority may exercise the right of eminent domain for the condemnation of private property or any right or interest therein for its use within the territorial limits defined." "The use of any property, or rights or interests therein, necessary or useful for the purposes of the Author-

> ity," says the act, "is here by declared to be a superior and permanent right and necessity, and a more necessary use and purpose than the use or purpose to which such property has already been appropriated or dedicated." And the act further provided that "all such property, and the income therefrom, are exempt from all taxation by any state or by any county, city and county, city, municipality, district, political subdivision or public corporation thereof."[19]

In the ensuing years, the agreement with the State Parks Commission was adopted "by mandate," as the Parks Commission had stated, and most of the ensuing talk about the tramway and facilities had quit mentioning terms like "skiers" and "winter sports enthusiasts" for terms like "tourists" and "sightseers." In short, in the minds of the opposition movement, this project was simply a way for Palm Springs to become a year-round resort to the benefit of Palm Springs promoters and a few others.

Argument 3

The Purpose and Reason for the Authority Are Based Upon Misrepresentation

This argument was further divided into the use of the area for skiing and the accessibility of the region for the general public. With regard to the suitability of the area for skiing, opponents pointed out that for the 15 years that the tramway had been promoted, it was done almost solely with the skier and winter sports enthusiast in mind:

> When finished, [the tramway] will permit snow sports enthusiasts in winter and fishermen in summer to ascend to the mountain heights in less than 15 minutes. Some of the best skiing areas in Southern California are to be found on the slopes of Mt. San Jacinto.[20]

According to the opponents of the tramway, though, that sentiment was only accepted by the proponents of the project. Skiers, both professional and otherwise, thought little of the potential of Mt. San Jacinto:

After on-the-spot study, the experts . . . . report that the terrain of San Jacinto is extremely rugged, the west slope being heavily timbered and the north, east, and south slopes dropping precipitously from rocky, knife-edge ridges to an upland shelf scarred with ravines and giant boulders, whence it catapults over immense precipices to the desert floor 8,000 feet below. Moreover, the steep and rocky upper 1,500 feet is absolutely unskiable.

The only potentially available ski terrain in the entire San Jacinto area is the rough, partly open slopes between the 8,000- and 9,000-foot levels, approximately 500 feet above and below the level of the upper terminal of the proposed tramway. But these slopes are 2 miles distant from the terminal, necessitating further transportation facilities not presently planned. There are no up-ski facilities on these slopes nor are any planned. And most importantly, these slopes which face south and southeast require a minimum of 6 feet of snow for safe skiing, a depth which rarely occurs even after heavy snowfalls.

This project, according to reliable winter sports surveys, by the very nature of its location can never be anything more than a sight-seeing attraction. By no sound measure can it

Postcard view of a skier in the San Jacinto Mountains (Author's collection).

> ever be a practical skiing development. As the Southern Area Planning committee in a joint report with the State Chamber of Commerce Winter Sports Committee emphasized: "It is the well-considered opinion of veteran skiers that the best skiable areas on Mt. San Jacinto are inferior to already available areas in Southern California."[21]

In addition to countering the proponents' promotion of the area for skiing, opponents also took them to task for calling the region "inaccessible." Proponents of the tramway had often indicated that the region was only accessible by the heartiest of individuals, and not really the general public. A rather tongue-in-cheek example was penned as a letter to the editor in the Los Angeles *Times* by Aaron Shum:

> If the area is so beautiful and awe inspiring then we do need a tramway. Then you, I and the less hardy portion of the population (about 99%) have a chance to see and enjoy this magnificence. Why save it for just a few hardy mountain climbers? Or for a "nature boy"?
>
> And how would a narrow tramway, a good hotel, and a planned and restricted recreation area spoil such a vast area? That is like saying that the good roads and fine hotel at Yosemite made it into an amusement park.
>
> How many of us would like to see the roads at Yosemite destroyed and the hotels boarded up so that members of the Sierra Club, Izaak Walton League and the Wilderness Society can hike in and have it all to themselves?
>
> After the project is completed there will still be plenty of room (more than they'll ever need) for the Sierra Club hikers, for the mountaineers, for the nature boys and girls and for the wild life enthusiast. Also for the antisocial and the maladjusted who want to "get away from it all."[22]

This sentiment was countered by indicating that several roads now existed into the mountains which made Idyllwild, the State Park, and National Forest much more accessible than it ever was. The Pines-to-Palms Highway had been opened between Indio and Keen Camp in

Postcard view of the Pines-to-Palms Highway by Stephen Willard, 1939 (Author's collection).

1932.[23] A new, vastly improved Banning-Idyllwild Road made accessing the mountains much simpler and safer from the San Gorgonio Pass area. The Hemet-Idyllwild Road, the first of the major ones into the mountains, had been improved in the late 1920s and had been welcoming people since 1929. "In fact," Harry James said, "the only parts of the state park which are not accessible are the dangerous cliffs of the escarpment toward Palm Springs – a dangerous area even for experienced mountaineers."[24] Furthermore, he cited a 1949 U.S. Forest Service description of the San Jacinto Primitive Area that tells prospective visitors, "The San Jacinto Primitive Area offers a splendid opportunity to both foot and horse travelers to explore its primitive places at a low cost and *easy accessibility*."[25] (Emphasis added)

Argument 4

The Proponents Never Mention Summer Use of the Area

As seen above, all mention of use of the facilities up to this point had been about winter sports. The opponents reasoned that such an effort and expense to construct a tramway could not be justified for only a few months' use, but there was never any mention of what the facilities would be used for in non-winter months. The implication, here, is that the tramway was there to establish a foothold in the mountains for Palm Springs interests so that they could establish a tax-free resort available year-round. Since at this time, Palm Springs still shut down during the summer, it was surmised that with facilities in the mountains, owned and operated by Palm Springs' interests, the town would become a year-round resort, thus enriching its promoters. This sentiment was summed up by attorney Braeme Gigas, "the tramway is merely an excuse and an entering wedge for the real object, the construction of a multimillion dollar resort in the primitive area."

Postcard view of the Palm Springs resort, 1945 (Author's collection).

Chapter 7 Endnotes

1. California Legislature, A. B. 1239, 56th session (1945).
2. Knowland, Joseph R., President of the California State Parks Commission, as quoted in the Palm Springs *Limelight*, March 7, 1946.
3. Fleming, April-June 1949, p. 25.
4. California Legislature, A. B. 1337, 58th session (1949).
5. Palm Springs *Limelight News*, January 25, 1949. The last sentence, though, failed to take into account that the Authority was still licensed to build all manner of ski and winter sports facilities at the top of the tram.
6. *The Desert Sun*, February 4, 1949.
7. It did at least make it to the Assembly's committee of Government Efficiency and Economy in March. Because of this, Earl Coffman was forced to go to Sacramento to answer for the Authority. Calling the attempt "screwball legislation," Coffman belittled the effort but bemoaned the fact that he would have to make the trip regardless. (*The Desert Sun*, March 1, 1949).
8. According to the website of The Wilderness Society, in 1935, a group of preservationists formed The Wilderness Society to save some of America's dwindling wildlands. At the time, forests and other public lands were mainly seen as resources for logging, mining and other development. Fighting to conserve the wildlands is considered a revolutionary idea. (https://www.wilderness.org/about-us/our-team/our-history, accessed December 8, 2021).
9. James, Winter 1949-1950, p. 5.
10. Hall, 1902, p. 14.
11. Momyer, Joe, as quoted in James, Winter 1949-1950, p. 7.
12. James, Winter 1949-1950, p. 7.
13. Olmstead, Frederick Law, as cited in Fleming, October 1949, p. 8.
14. Drury, Newton, memo to Joseph R. Knowland dated June 12, 1937, cited in Fleming, October 1949, p. 9. This, of course, flew right in the face of Knowland's approval of the tramway project during the postwar years.
15. Fleming, October 1949, p. 10, as cited in James, Winter 1949-1950, p. 10.
16. James, Winter 1949-1950, p. 11
17. It will be remembered that this situation was the basis for the original opposition by Riverside County to the creation of such an entity.
18. James, Winter 1949-1950, p. 11.

19. *Ibid*, pp. 11-12.

20. Los Angeles *Times*, January 1, 1949.

21. Hauk, A. Andrew et al, March 1, 1949, p. 2. This sentiment was mentioned to the author by John Watson, the present historian for the Far West Ski Association. He indicated that while there are some areas suitable for skiing on Mt. San Jacinto, they are nowhere near the mountain station of the tramway (Watson, John, personal communication with the author, December 9, 2021).

22. Shum, Aaron. Los Angeles *Times* Letters to the Editor, May 4, 1949.

23. This highway was another sore spot with the promoters of Palm Springs. Ever since the idea of a road between the desert and mountains was conceived in the late 1910s, it was always envisioned to lead from Keen Camp (near present-day Mountain Center) to Vandeventer Flats, then turn north and travel down Palm Canyon and into downtown Palm Springs. Because of the diligence of two men – J. Win Wilson of the Indio *Date Palm* newspaper and Wilson Howell of Ribbonwood, plus the reluctance of the Agua Caliente people to open Palm Canyon to the motoring public, this never happened, and instead, the road led farther east along the route it has today. This greatly upset the promoters of Palm Springs who had wanted the famed Pines-to-Palms Highway to lead to their city. For more information on the development of the Pines-to-Palms Highway, see Lech, Steve, *For Tourism and a Good Night's Sleep – J. Win Wilson, Wilson Howell, and the Beginnings of the Pines-to-Palms Highway.*

24. James, Winter 1949-1950, p. 13.

25. *Ibid.*

Chapter 8

Further Delays

A vast desert-mountain empire is in the making!

Oliver Jaynes, as quoted in The Desert Sun, *February 4, 1949.*

Please do not consider this "California's Problem." The construction of this tramway into the San Jacinto State Park is not only a breach of faith with those citizens who have contributed and worked to build up the California State Park system, but it gives encouragement to those who would invade state parks, national parks, or wilderness areas in any state.

Federation of Outdoor Clubs letter, March 20, 1953.

At the beginning of 1949, most of Palm Springs and the region was optimistic that construction of the much-ballyhooed tramway would start, probably by year's end. In bringing his readers up to speed on the status of the project, *Desert Sun* editor Oliver B. Jaynes, an unabashed proponent of the project, indicated that due to the Mt. San Jacinto Winter Park Authority having no money of its own, progress had been at a standstill up to a few months before. More studies were needed and more data had to be gathered in order to complete the engineering and bid documents. Fortunately, the Authority had been able to convince the American Steel and Wire Company to advance the funds needed to complete the studies, and they were well underway by the beginning of the year.[1]

> The authority has no preliminary operating funds. This handicap has been the cause of most of the delays. The steel company has advanced most of the money for field work – and the Palm Springs chamber of commerce has helped out a little.[2]

Once these studies were completed and submitted, the Authority could get a firm cost estimate for the project, and then go about selling revenue bonds to raise the projected $5,000,000 it would take to build the project.[3]

Postcard view of the Tramview Trail Park, mid 1950s. This was one of many such places to adopt the tramway name (Author's collection).

As an indicator of the optimistic mood in Palm Springs with the impending tramway, several advertisements for and articles about real estate transactions appear during this time. Real estate, especially around the Chino Canyon area where the tramway would be built, was a hot commodity. This, of course, did not go unnoticed by the tram's opposition, who had always thought the tram project a means of boosting real estate values within the city.

The data was slow in coming, and since the Authority was operating by the good graces of the American Steel and Wire Company, it was in no position to make demands that the work be hastened. By June, it was time for another much-publicized two-day horseback trip to the site of the mountain station, wherein several of the engineers came along to tout the project.

Delays continued to plague the project throughout the summer and fall of 1949. By September, when yet another club was being apprised of the status of the project, promoter Henry Harper had to acknowledge that the preliminary estimate had risen from $1.5 million originally to approximately $5 million. "The problem, is how high can the Authority go and pay off? Naturally, there is a ceiling" he lamented.[4]

Gordon Bannerman, one of many engineers working on the project, finally came to the Authority on October 11 with what was generally agreed to be the final engineering report for the project. With that, it was hoped, a firm cost estimate could be ascertained so that bonds could begin to be sold. With the completion of the engineering work in October, though, came yet another delay. A major steel strike hit most of the east coast in October and November of that year, throwing the price of steel into flux and with it any hope for a firm estimate for the project.

By December, labor issues had been resolved, and some firm numbers for a cost estimate were available. So sure were the promoters of the project that Earl Coffman, chair of the Authority, held a news conference on December 18 where he confidently predicted that construction would begin in February, 1950, and the tram would be available for the Christmas season of 1951.[5]

Horseback trek into the San Jacinto Mountains, c. 1930s. (Idyllwild Area Historical Society photo).

In fact, Coffman's confidence was quite high. Just the next week, reports were surfacing that the new, most up-to-date cost estimate for the project stood at $9 million – nearly twice as much as the previous high estimate. "With the final estimated price on the big Mt. San Jacinto Aerial Tramway now standing at better than $9 million, can the Tramway pay out?" asked the *Desert Sun* newspaper.[6] Backers of the project acknowledged that the new estimate was very high. In fact, it was near the upper limit of what many thought could be recouped by the tram.

Supporters turned to their own estimates of traffic showing, in their words, "millions" of people traveling within six miles of the project site per year. They believed that many of these people could be diverted to Palm Springs to view or ride the newest wonder. They also cited additional studies of the Mt. Cannon Aerial Tramway in Franconia Notch, New Hampshire, showing that many people traveling within a large radius of that tramway could be diverted to it. Even more reassuring was the fact that the Mt. Cannon Aerial Tramway was located nearly seven hours away from the nearest major population center, whereas Palm Springs was but three hours distant from Los Angeles.[7]

Due to the inflated costs, financing the project was paramount as 1949 became 1950. By February, 1950, backers were looking to the U.S. Government's Reconstruction Finance Corporation as a means of possible funds. Inroads were made towards applying for funds, but the RFC, which had been formed at the height of the Great Depression, was by this time winding down its operation and beginning to be investigated by Senators who believed the organization corrupt. In short, an appeal to the RFC for funds went nowhere.

While questions of funding continued, another major hurdle loomed large for the tramway, and the opponents knew it. Still to be obtained was a right-of-way across lands maintained by the U. S. Forest Service. While this prospect had been simmering for quite some time (see Chapter 9), it was coming to a head and stood to be the one portion of the entire project that could derail or entirely doom the tramway. And of course, it would mean more delays.

Hikers approach the summit of Mt. San Jacinto, c. 1930s. (Idyllwild Area Historical Society photo).

Chapter 8 Endnotes

1. Jaynes, Oliver B. "The Publisher's Corner." *The Desert Sun*, February 4, 1949.
2. *Ibid.* Per the original enabling legislation, the Authority was not allowed to sell bonds prior to having construction documents and a firm construction estimate in hand.
3. Approximately $61,500,000 in 2023 dollars.
4. *The Desert Sun*, September 13, 1949.
5. *The Desert Sun*, December 20, 1949.
6. *The Desert Sun*, December 27, 1949.
7. *Ibid.*

Chapter 9

Further Opposition and the Land Exchange

There is a lot of land in this big country of ours where commercial exploiters can play with their engineering stunts.

Devereux Butcher, testimony before the United States Forest Service's hearing on the right-of-way application by the Mt. San Jacinto Winter Park Authority, April 20, 1950.

What the tramway will mean for Palm Springs is unfathomable at this time. Nevertheless, the skeptics of many years standing are now shouting from the rooftops: "Well, I told you so – never doubted for a minute that we would have the tramway. No sir-eeee!"

Bill Rashall, Reporter for The Desert Sun, *April 12, 1954.*

With two big defeats behind them, opponents of the Tramway began to look inwards and realized that their biggest weakness was a lack of coordination. Harry James was doing what he thought he could as one man, members of the Sierra Club were writing letters and trying to get members at the state level to join in, and other organizations were similarly acting alone in their own opposition to the proposed tramway. In an attempt to unite the opposition, Harry James called a meeting of many of these groups at his Trailfinders School in Altadena.

This effort did bring together several of the various factions, at least so that they could and would talk among themselves and provide a more united front. One outcome of the meeting was that Harry James would no longer be at the forefront in the fight against the tramway. In fact, that torch was soon given to the local chapter of the Sierra Club in Riverside. Several of their members, including A. J. Twogood of Riverside, Joe Momyer of San Bernardino, and Ken Buck of Riverside, formed a special subcommittee of the chapter devoted to just the Tramway issue. In April, 1949, this subcommittee, in consultation with others, opted to attack the issue on two fronts. First, despite earlier losses in the same vein, they would concentrate on the remaining agreement the Authority needed, namely, one for a right-of-way across the National Forest land in Section 12.[1] They would also muster legal

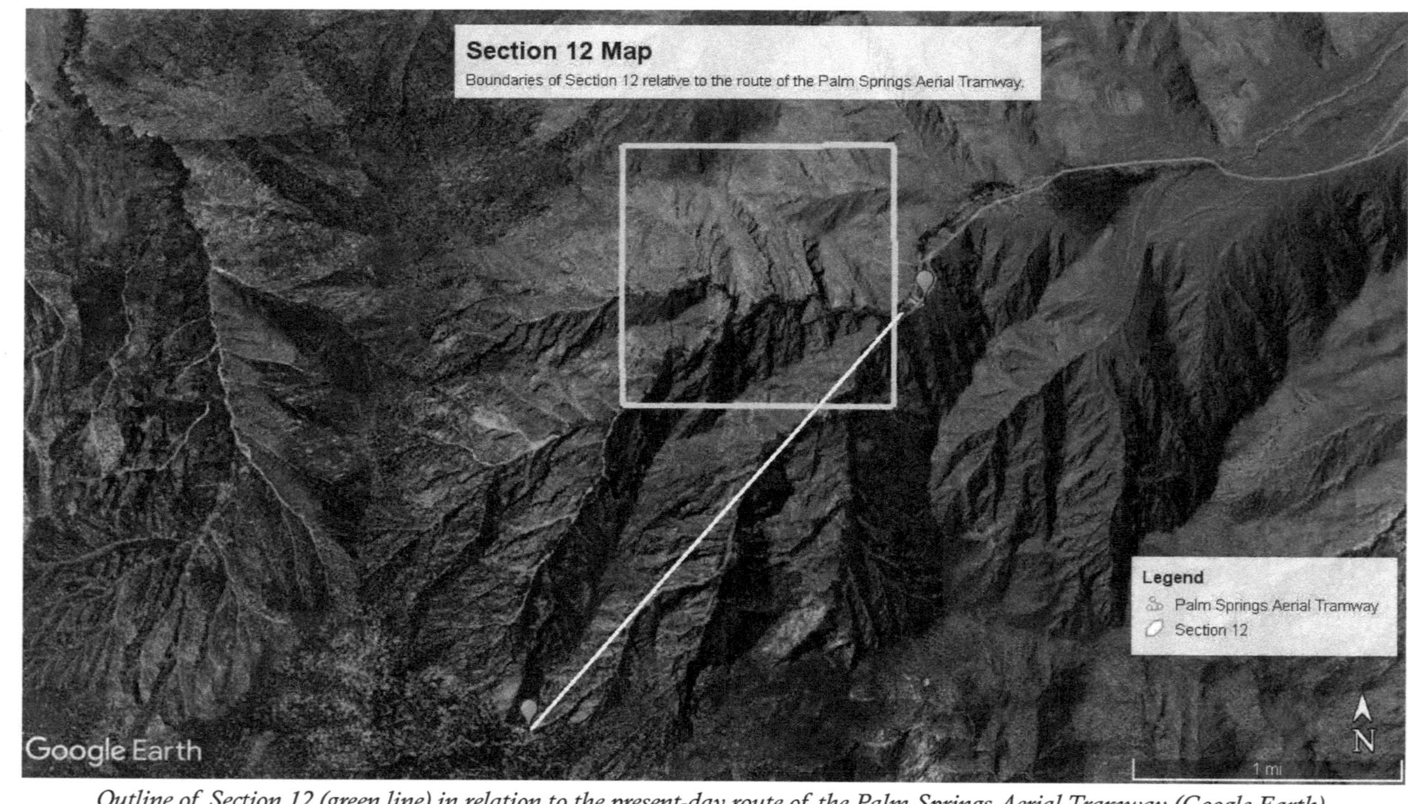

Outline of Section 12 (green line) in relation to the present-day route of the Palm Springs Aerial Tramway (Google Earth).

forces to challenge both the constitutionality of the Authority itself and of its ability to sell unlimited bonds, the main method of financing the project.

Since the application for a right-of-way over the National Forest land was still not formalized, and hence no hearing date had been set, the group had some time to concentrate on both promoting their main arguments against the tramway and to have legal counsel investigate the constitutionality of the Authority.

In short, many in the Sierra Club believed that the original intent of the state park was an agreement wherein the State would maintain the San Jacinto Mountains as a primitive area. They argued that the original bonds that were sold to create the State Park were, in effect, a referendum measure, and "the legislature would have no authority to interfere with the program that had thus been set up by the people."[2] The legal opinion of this reasoning came back quickly and not in the Club's favor. It was stated that, "the park was state property and the authority a state agency, [which] protected it against constitutional provisions forbidding the legislative grant of special privileges to any corporation, and it seemed unlikely that winter sports development would be considered an improper use for lands purchased with funds from the 1928 bond act.[3]

With a potential legal challenge knocked out of their arsenal, the opponents of the tram spent 1949 shoring up their arguments, disseminating them to anyone who would listen, and preparing for the next opportunity, namely the right-of-way hearing before the United States Forest Service. Unfortunately, the USFS was tight-lipped about when that would occur, and delays on the part of the proponents kept it from happening until the spring of 1950.

So throughout 1949, opposition to the tramway grew, and knowledge of the tramway project similarly grew as Harry James, Joe Momyer, and many others sought to educate the public as to what exactly was in store for the Mt. San Jacinto wilderness if the tramway project was allowed to proceed. Joe Momyer headed a consortium of people who wrote essays regarding the need for wilderness areas in Southern California. He collected many more than were actually published, and those that were published were done so mainly in the Sierra Club Bulletin. As others pointed out, this publication was largely "preaching to the choir" when it came to trying to drum up support for the opposition. Although many additional copies of these Bulletin essays were printed, in an age before mass media and the internet, there were only so many places they could be disseminated. Regardless, Momyer's essay, "Wilderness Recreation for a Metropolitan Area," and Guy Fleming's "Should We Cherish and Maintain the San Jacinto Wild Area?" made passionate pleas for maintaining the greater San Jacinto Mountains area in a strict wilderness condition, one that was, in their minds, diminishing rapidly.[4]

When it came time for a public hearing on the granting of the right-of-way to the Mt. San Jacinto Winter Park Authority by the U.S. Forest Service, many people were caught off guard. Although it was customary to allow a 90-day notice for such hearings, when the April 20, 1950 date was announced, less than half of that time had been allotted. This created a minor panic among the opposition leaders, many of whom were hoping to continue to build on the groundswell of opposition seen throughout 1949. Instead, they had to act and act presently.

Joe Momyer, who had coordinated the efforts of outlining the arguments, appealed to dozens of newspapers throughout Riverside County and the larger region. His efforts were met with some success, but several newspapers were solidly for the project, especially within Riverside County. In fact, much of Riverside County was behind the project, including most newspapers, chambers of commerce, and a number of civic groups.

Still, Momyer and the others did have some success in getting their message across, and were able to get several letters written to USFS officials and others pleading their case. As April 20, 1950, approached, both sides were gearing up for a major confrontation.[5]

The purpose of the April 20 meeting was to take public input for the question of whether the United States Forest Service should grant a right-of-way for the tramway over lands controlled by that agency. This mainly included the portion of the cableway nearest the proposed Valley Station. As proposed, the tramway would cross a portion of Section 12, Township 4 South, Range 3 East, and required the right-of-way to be granted.

With both sides having had lots of time to rally their supporters, no doubt was left in anyone's mind that the April 20 hearing would be a large affair. "Tram hearing should draw full house today. 'Standing Room Only' signs are expected to be out this morning for the U. S. Forest Service's public hearing on the controversial Mt. San Jacinto

Aerial Tramway" noted the Riverside *Enterprise*.[6] The hearing, held in the Board of Supervisors' meeting room in the Riverside County courthouse, lasted two days.[7]

Both sides knew that this hearing, and the ultimate decision by the U. S. Department of the Interior, would probably be a "do-or-die" moment for the tramway. Most of the engineering studies completed to this point indicated that not only was the Chino Canyon route the best route, it was also the most practical one for such a venture. Tramway proponents needed this right-of-way in order to fulfill their ability to construct the project. Similarly, the opponents saw this as their best opportunity to defeat the tramway proposal. In their minds, the U. S. Forest Service was much more aligned with their convictions. Since the opponents had already opted (out of necessity) to take their fight to a more national level, the hearing before the USFS seemed to be their best shot at getting the project killed, hopefully once and for all.

Over the two-day hearing, 89 people appeared before the USFS representatives, chaired by Regional Forester Perry A. Thompson. By a roughly 2-to-1 ratio, opponents of the tramway outnumbered proponents.[8] Chief speaker for the tramway advocates on the first day was Henry Lockwood, the attorney for the Mt. San Jacinto Winter Park Authority. On the second day, Earl Coffman led the advocacy for the tram. Both men, together with others, laid out a five-point argument for constructing the proposed tramway:

1. By constructing the tramway, the natural wonders of the San Jacinto Mountains, State Park, and Primitive Areas would be opened to the public for far more people to enjoy. In its present state, their argument went, only a few hearty souls could enjoy the region – those who can hike or afford horses to take them there. The tramway would allow rich and poor, firm and infirm, young and old the ability to partake of the region's scenic wonders.
2. The portion of Federal land in question was very small compared to the entire area. Also, the area being proposed for a right-of-way was extremely rugged and in essence unusable for recreational purposes. Furthermore, allowing access into the area via a tramway would almost certainly negate the need for a road to the area, which would have a far worse impact on the wilderness than a tramway.

3. The Winter Park Authority Act was an act of the State of California, and as such it was a mandate from the State for construction. The Act had been approved fully four times (although only signed into law once), and no political opposition was brought forth at that time.
4. Construction of the tramway would greatly aid in providing more recreational opportunities to Southern California's burgeoning population. With the regional population set to increase greatly, it would be more and more important to offer recreational opportunities for them.
5. The tramway would be a boost for the region's economy. Not only would it employ some 200 people on a regular basis, the argument went, many believed that such a unique entity would boost the recreation economy throughout all of Southern California.[9]

Opposition to the tram was led by Guy Fleming on Day 1 and Joe Momyer on Day 2. Together, these two men, along with many other speakers, outlined the main arguments against the tram, most of which had been stated and restated many times at meetings, other hearings, and in letters and articles. Conservation of wild areas and the riskiness of the tram proposal were the main points to their arguments, which can be broken down as such:

1. Back in the 1930s, a definite commitment was made to manage both the Forest Service's primitive area and the State's park as wilderness area;
2. Southern California's burgeoning population needed a wilderness area as a tonic, not another commercial scheme.
3. Allowing the tramway and ancillary uses to be constructed, and the ensuing swarms of people that would result from their use, would destroy the region's wilderness condition.
4. The Mt. San Jacinto Winter Park Authority was essentially an arm of the powerful commercial interests of Palm Springs;
5. Because the Winter Park Authority was now basing much of their argument on tourists and tourism, it had abandoned its original intent – that of creating a winter sports area – and was going against its legislative "mandate."[10]

In addition, members of the Sierra Club stated that the tram itself and the approvals it would need constituted a foot in the door for other projects to further degrade the wilderness area. All of the machinery, buildings, pavement, and other improvements that would have to be made to the upper region would leave an indelible mark on the land. These improvements would have to be constructed at some point in order to make the tramway viable.[11] In a similar vein, because the tramway's viability was anything but assured, many on the opposing side worried about the prospect of the wilderness area being strewn with the ruins of the failed tramway. Citing evidence of this in the case of the Mt. Lowe Railway, several people asked that if the right-of-way was granted, it was done so only with the provision for a bond to be used to return the area to a natural state.[12]

In keeping with the zeitgeist of the post-war times, arguments were made that the proposed tramway was an undemocratic proposal for the following reasons:

1. Assurances had been made, and public and private monies spent, on the creation of the park and wilderness area with the assurances that they would remain as wilderness areas;
2. The proposal in essence would use public lands for private gain;
3. The Winter Park Authority Act had been approved at a time when most of the contemporary opponents were away at war, therefore not having the possibility of stating their opposition at the time; and,
4. The intent of the proposal, ever-changing from one of winter sports development to tourism development, sought to increase real estate values in Palm Springs, thus using the development of a public park for private gains.[13]

Finally, other speakers and letter writers approached the subject from a much broader perspective. The tramway proposal was one of several nationwide that was seeking to somehow compromise what had been established (at least in the minds of preservationists). They reasoned that if the San Jacinto application was allowed, it would set a precedent for others. On this subject, Devereux Butcher, the executive secretary and field representative for the National Parks Association from 1942-1957, postulated the following:

> It is not enough to consider alone the injury to the Mount San Jacinto Primitive Area and the Mount San Jacinto State Park, although this in itself is very serious. We must recognize the far reaching effects that this proposed commercial development would have. If half a dozen men can wield sufficient power to convince their legislators that state park policy should be put aside to allow them to use state park lands for a special purpose, why cannot similar groups do likewise in other state parks? And, since what affects the natural beauty and primitive wilderness character of the Mount San Jacinto Park will also adversely affect the adjoining Forest Service Primitive Area, who would dare to say that attempts will not be made by other special interests to break down the federal system of primitive and wilderness areas throughout the West?
>
> The bill authorizing tramway construction gives a long list of structures and facilities to be built on state park land for the accommodation of tramway riders. It is our understanding that the Winter Park Authority does not intend to disturb the park landscape with such structures. The Authority may have this intention, and may adhere strictly to it, but what can we expect of future members of the Authority? A new administration could abandon former policies, if it wished.
>
> There is a lot of land in this big country of ours where commercial exploiters can play with their engineering stunts. What land remains untouched is already far too little to meet the growing demand for wilderness recreation.[14]

Public testimony ended on April 21, 1950, but there was still time to be heard, because public written comments would still be accepted for a couple more weeks. Meanwhile, Perry Thompson, the Regional Forester, began to develop his recommendation about the Authority's application. The application for right-of-way across State of California territory was relatively simple, but the application for the right to cross Federal territory would be a whole other issue.

From the outset, the Federal government wanted to stay out of the controversy surrounding the tramway application. Issues brought up on San Jacinto Mountain could have precedent over all areas of

Present-day view of the Palm Springs Tramway from the Valley Station. Section 12 begins just past the road at the bottom of the picture (Author's photo).

Forest Service authority, and the Federal government did not want to get embroiled in what was in essence a private development proposal. Furthermore, the portion of the route the proposed tramway would take amounted to the corner of one section of land on the periphery of an area controlled by the Forest Service. In addition, not only was the amount of land in question small, it was quite unusable from a geographic and recreational standpoint. Nearly all rockface with steep sides, the portion of Section 12 was hardly an area worthy of recreational amenities.

Another point facing the Federal government was the fact that, despite agreeing with the State government that the San Jacinto Mountains area would remain in a primitive state, the State of California had already authorized the intrusion of the proposed tramway. This left the Federal government in the position of being the "bad guy" with the Authority's right-of-way application – they could approve it and bring on the ire of the conservationist contingency, or they could deny it and go against the wishes of the State of California. All of this weighed heavily on Perry Thompson.

The application for a right-of-way had been requested under a statute from March 3, 1899 allowing for rights-of-way for "wagon roads and railroads." The short statute indicates that "In the form provided by existing law the Secretary of the Interior may file and approve surveys and plats of any right of way for a wagon road, railroad, or other highway over and across any national forest when in his judgement the public interests will not be injuriously affected thereby."[15] In essence, the Authority reasoned that the tramway would fit into the definition of "other highway" for its purposes.

After considering all factors, on June 15, 1950, Regional Forester Perry Thompson submitted his detailed report to Washington D.C.[16] In it, Thompson seems to have sided with the conservationists in his tone, but ultimately made a recommendation that would have removed the US Forest Service from the controversy. His recommendation was that the enabling legislation for the Mt. San Jacinto Winter Park Authority be amended to make its territory of influence match only areas under the control of the State of California, and to the south half of Section 12.

Thompson noted that much of the testimony by pro-tramway advocates seemed to advance the cause for its effects on local business. That did not sit well with him, given that the U. S. Forest Service was being asked to approve an incursion into a primitive area for the sake of business. On that topic, Thompson was not convinced that the Authority's plans were financially sound. The issue of financing the tramway, and the sale of bonds, was still sketchy. He reasoned that there was a better-than-average chance that all or part of the tramway could be built, then abandoned for financial reasons, all the while leaving the permanent scars of a failed project.

Along those lines, he noted that the State of California had already been granted an exemption from any financial responsibility for the tram, so no monies would be coming from that entity should the tram fail. On the other hand, the Authority's enabling legislation did allow that entity to accept federal, state or other grants. He went on to find that, "A reasonable supposition is that the motive for the inclusion of such provisions in the law was fear that the project might not prove self-supporting and in that event the promoters would be able to use their demonstrated talents in the field of public affairs and secure public funds--anywhere they could succeed in getting them--to bail out the project."[17]

If the project did need to be bailed out sometime in the future, then granting a right-of-way could hardly be termed in the public's interest as the law mandates. If the scars remained on Mt. San Jacinto, along with the remnants of a failed tramway project, the wilderness value of the San Jacinto Primitive Area would be destroyed. With that, Thompson also recommended that the Authority's ability to accept funds from the Federal government be revoked.

In the end, on November 3, 1950, Secretary of the Interior Oscar Chapman denied the Authority's application for a right-of-way across Section 12. Thompson's recommendations had weighed heavily in Chapman's decision, together with the Federal government's unwillingness to get involved in an explosive local matter. Luckily for him, Chapman had a convenient technicality upon which to base his denial, namely the inapplicability of the 1899 rules governing rights-of-way and the fact that an aerial tramway did not meet the requirements of a wagon road, railroad, or highway. Once handed down, this denial made no one happy.

Obviously, proponents of the tramway were enraged by the denial. Hundreds of thousands of dollars had already been spent by the Authority[18] and several private companies, the latter of which were hoping to be selected as the construction company. "The Mt. San Jacinto Winter Park aerial tramway will be built!" stated Earl Coffman, Chairman of the Winter Park Authority.[19] He went on to say, "the

Cover of the February, 1950 Palm Springs Villager dedicated to the Palm Springs Tramway (Palm Springs Life archive).

state of California handed the Authority a mandate to erect the tramway and it will be erected. . . . . We have overcome many obstacles in the past to get as far as we have and the ruling the solicitor for the department of the interior that its secretary cannot grant us a right-of-way will not stop the construction of the tramway."[20] Harry Harper, a Riverside resident who acted in a volunteer capacity as a spokesman for the Authority in western Riverside County, speculated that Congressional action was not out of the question. "There are so many people in California who are interested in [the tramway] that it certainly won't stop here." He went on to say that some engineers working on the project had told him that there were alternative routes the tramway could take, potentially going around Section 12, but that they would be longer and more costly.[21]

The tramway opponents were initially happy the right-of-way had been denied. It didn't take long, though, for them to see that their elation was ill-warranted. As Earl Coffman put it, "the conservationist angle over which a lengthy hearing was held in Riverside did not enter the picture or influence the secretary of interior in his decision."[22] This did not escape Joe Momyer and others, too, who saw that the denial was on a technicality – i.e. the ruling that the tramway is not a highway. The Forest Service's denial had nothing to do with conservation issues, opening up the San Jacinto Primitive Area to development, or any of the myriad other reasons put forth by the opposition to effect a denial of the Authority's application. Joe Momyer, among others, indicated that,

> It is certainly important to note that the Secretary denied this application purely on the technical grounds of lack of authority, and that no permanent blocking of the tramway plans results. Since no fundamental decision as to public policy has been gained, we can expect the tramway proponents to make still further efforts to force the project through. Certainly it is wise to recognize the fact that we have antagonists who are both determined and resourceful. Although the Secretary's decision and the war demand for metals will result in serious delay for them, all conservationists and friends of Mt. San Jacinto should be alert for further moves on the part of the Winter Park Authority.[23]

"Further moves" is exactly what the Authority had in mind. Realizing that they were denied based upon a technicality that could easily be overcome, members of the Authority, especially their lead attorney Henry Lockwood, began discussions with management-level members of the Forest Service. This included going all the way to the top – Lyle. F. Watts, Chief of the U. S. Forest Service. Indicating that the tramway backers were willing to go to Congress[24] if necessary to effect a change, Lockwood pressed the Forest Service for a compromise on the right-of-way issue.

After about six weeks of back-and-forth discussions between Watts and the tram promoters, Watts issued a letter to the Authority outlining several conditions under which the Forest Service would give a positive recommendation to a land exchange to remove the south ½ of Section 12 from the San Jacinto Primitive Area. This occasion also gave Watts and the Forest Service the opportunity to remove themselves from the controversy of the tramway proposal altogether. In short, Watts demanded that;

1. The Authority submit and have approved an amended Mount San Jacinto Winter Park Authority Act which completely separates the authorized operating area of the Authority from the San Jacinto Primitive Area;
2. The Authority submit an application for a land exchange which includes the following stipulation to protect the Primitive Area;
    a. "The San Jacinto Winter Park Authority stipulates that its program of development and operation of the San Jacinto Aerial Tramway and other facilities will not necessitate requests for any invasion whatsoever of the San Jacinto Primitive Area, including access roads for construction, water developments or any other improvements, and stipulates further that it will not request any uses in the primitive area."
3. The Authority will offer to the United States a tract of either private or State-owned land within a primitive area that has an equal or greater value to that of the south ½ of Section 12 in exchange for the south ½ of Section 12.[25]

This set of conditions would turn over the disputed land in Section 12 in exchange for removing the operating area of the Authority from the Primitive Area and ensuring that no aspect of the tramway would invade the Primitive Area. If these conditions were met, the U. S. Forest Service would be completely removed from the tramway proposal, which is what they wanted in the first place.

At the beginning of 1951, proponents of the tramway were facing mounting obstacles to its construction. First, the land exchange between the Authority and the United States Forest Service had to be completed, and that required new legislation. Second, the United States' entry into the Korean conflict meant steel and other materials would be severely rationed for non-defense industries, making it nearly impossible to begin construction even if all permits had been secured.

A third obstacle was looming also. The original approval they had received from the California State Parks Commission was set to expire on January 1, 1952. This meant that in addition to all the other work they had to do, they would also have to appear again in front of the Commission to seek an extension, and the opposition would have yet another opportunity to air their points and potentially derail, if not defeat, the tramway project.

Extending the approval of the Parks Commission was the first item to be taken up. Testimony was taken by the Parks Commission on March 16, 1951. Ken Buck, of the Sierra Club, indicated that their position would be that,

> The building is not feasible because of steel shortages, that costs have increased five-fold since the tramway bill was authorized, that in the two years since the contract was made the Authority had not been able to get a right of way from the government on which to build, and that no economic plan for the construction of the tramway has been made public.[26]

The arguments, though, did not sway the Parks Commission, which granted an extension of five years to the Authority for construction of the tramway.[27]

With the extension granted, thc Authority could now concentrate on the land exchange. Meetings held with the tramway proponents and California State Assemblyman John Babbage had resulted in an amendment to the Winter Park Authority Act which restated the section outlining the physical extent of the Authority, cutting approximately 12 square miles from the original area outlined in the 1945 act. Introduced on March 26 into the Assembly as AB 3391 by Assemblyman Babbage, the bill went through the process with little trouble. It was signed by Governor Warren on June 11, 1951.[28]

As for the opposition to the tramway, this latest opportunity to argue against the project was moot. Several in the anti-tramway camps thought about rallying a force to go to Sacramento, and others suggested yet another letter-writing campaign. However, these pursuits were quickly shot down. The Assembly Bill only sought to reduce the scope of the Winter Park Authority. Arguing against the tramway itself was completely against the point, since the legislation did not address the tramway per se. This point was made abundantly clear when one anti-tram advocate, John O'Kane of the Izaac Walton League, did make a pitch to the Assembly, only to be cut off by the chair indicating that his statements and arguments were not germane to the bill at hand. Therefore, the bill became law with little opposition.[29]

With the reduction of area under which the Authority could operate the tram and appurtenant uses, attention now turned to the actual negotiations for swapping land. Throughout the various changes over the years, the Authority had left itself control of two separate sections of land on the north face of Mt. San Jacinto, probably with the hopes that these could be used in exchange for the south half of Section 12. These were Sections 3 and 5, and were owned by the Palm Springs Water Company as part of their holdings for the waters in Falls Creek. Throughout 1951 and 1952, negotiations went back and forth between the Authority and the U. S. Forest Service, the latter of which was eager to make a deal that it could show was in the U. S. Government's best interest while also trying to assuage the conservationist opposition that they were not wholeheartedly "selling out" to the business interests behind the tramway proposal.

Due to some legal technicalities, Section 5 was taken out of the discussions, which left Section 3 with which to bargain. This is the ultimate deal that was brokered between the parties, and was applied for in late 1952. In February and March, 1953, public notice was given by the Regional Forester regarding the proposed land exchange. This became another point in which the opposition could make its case, but unfortunately, for whatever reason, the opposition was caught off-guard and had to mobilize quickly.[30]

Many of the same groups that formed the opposition wrote to the Regional Forester to demand that the land exchange be denied. The arguments used had not changed much, but the need to have the exchange denied was probably seen as the last and best hope to keep the tramway from materializing. The years 1952, 1953, and the early part of 1954 were consumed in negotiations and a lot of behind-the-scenes activities. The U. S. Forest Service seemed amenable to the exchange throughout the process. As negotiations continued, and it looked like the land exchange would go through, the subject of actually purchasing the property from the Palm Springs Water Company came up. Purchasing the land meant the Authority, which still had no money of its own, would have to lay out $5,000. The Authority, as usual, went to the public and asked for subscriptions from Palm Springs residents. Luckily for them, 10 replied with contributions of $500 each, which in turn allowed for the parcel to be purchased so it could be exchanged.[31]

As can be imagined, the tramway proposal lost a lot of its momentum during this time. Negotiations were, by necessity, handled in meetings that were not generally open to the public. The tramway proponents, though, were persistent, but also knew that construction of the tramway would not happen during the Korean conflict due to shortages of materials and the appropriation of materials for defense efforts. Luckily for them, these two items happened almost concurrently.

It didn't keep people from asking about the tramway proposal, though. While several of the backers would mention that it was continuing to be pushed, little was shown in the papers to keep the proposal in front of the public. Even Oliver Jaynes, the publisher of the *Desert Sun* newspaper and stalwart supporter of the tramway, had to editorialize about the absence of news on the project based on questions he was receiving:

> Another question frequently asked me: "What has happened to the tramway?" People still remember all the publicity given the projected tourist lift to the lofty heights of San Jacinto and wonder if it will ever be built. That's a question I can't answer. I wonder too . . . . . This seems to be the time, if ever, to get some action. It would be very interesting to know what is being done in the light of changed conditions. I would think from talking with Edward Bacon up in San Francisco that he doesn't believe the tramway will ever be built because

> it will cost so much now. He remembers when he and his associates offered to build it for $2,500,000. The last estimate was around ten million as I recall.[32]

It took until April, 1954, but in the end, Secretary of the Interior Douglas McKay approved the proposed land exchange, which took place on April 9. The Mt. San Jacinto Winter Park Authority would get ownership of the 326-acre south half of Section 12, and the U. S. Forest Service would get 600 acres that comprised Section 3 about two miles west of the tramway. McKay stated that "careful consideration" was given to a number of the protests lodged against the proposed land exchange, but that he felt the public interest would be best served by approving the transfer.[33] McKay's approval, however, was not without conditions. Alluding to Perry Thompson's recommendations of a few years ago, McKay made the stipulation that the Authority could not move into or use any part of the Mt. San Jacinto Primitive Area for the construction or operation of the tramway. This condition does not seem to have phased the promoters of the project.

McKay's condition may have been caused by, or simply fell into the hands of, one other effort that was being undertaken by Harry James during the land-transfer episode. Given the pervasive feeling that too much had already been accomplished on the tramway, and too much had already been spent, James and a few others pushed for a compromise effort on the project. In James' proposed compromise, opposition parties would concede to the tramway's construction, provided that all references to and approvals for winter sports facilities in the mountains be removed from the Authority's enabling legislation. This, in the view of many anti-tram advocates, would accomplish at least two things. One, the opposition would appear to be genuinely trying to effect an amicable solution to the issue at hand, and not always being there simply to say "no!" Second, by reducing the project to simply the tramway itself, it was felt that the project would no longer be economically viable. In approving only the tramway and nothing else, the backers would soon realize that to continue the push for it was economically untenable.

James proposed his idea to the Sierra Club, whose opposition to the tramway project was waning when it was becoming clear that the project had strong state support, and there were many other larger, more pressing issues for them to work on.[34] The Sierra Club refused to take up James' compromise position, leaving the opposition to the tramway to fend for themselves. This was a tremendous setback for James and his cohorts.

It is doubtful that the proponents of the tramway heard much of the compromise proposed by Harry James. Their focus was on the much-needed land swap that took up a great deal of time. Upon hearing the news of the land exchange approval, O. Earl Coffman remarked, "This is good news, indeed – now the way is clear for us to proceed!"[35] "I see no obstacle now that will prevent the construction of the tramway" he continued.[36] Now, according to Coffman, they could update the economic survey done by Coverdale and Colpitts in 1950 so that a financial prospectus could be prepared for the issuance of bonds. He figured this would take several months, but that if everything went well, construction of the tramway could begin in 1955, with a potential opening after two years of construction.[37]

The early 1950s were a very rocky time for the Aerial Tramway proponents, but in the end, they overcame the opposition and the obstacles so that by late 1954, Francis Crocker, Earl Coffman, and many others could exude the same enthusiasm that Coffman had projected to the media after final approval of the land exchange. In addition to their successes, the Korean conflict had ended in the summer of 1953, which removed the barrier to materiel that had been in effect for a few years. But the longer it took for the tramway to be built, the more the opposition to it was growing. Sure, the national groups were largely abandoning the arguments against it in lieu of other, more pressing (in their eyes) issues, but local opposition was taking hold in a way it hadn't yet. New players would enter the arena as 1953 turned to 1954, and with them new tactics would be deployed.

Chapter 9 Endnotes

1. In non-survey terms, this is the lowest or northernmost portion of the tramway, nearest the Valley Station.
2. Davis, August 1973, p. 249.
3. *Ibid.*
4. Momyer, Joe. "Wilderness Recreation for a Metropolitan Area." Sierra Club Bulletin, Vol. 34, No. 8; September, 1949, and Fleming, Guy. "Should We Cherish and Maintain the San Jacinto Wild Area?" Sierra Club Bulletin, Vol. 34, No. 9; October, 1949. These two essays, together with Fleming's "The Mount San Jacinto Tramway Scheme" are reproduced as Appendix D.
5. Two forceful editorials appeared in the Riverside *Enterprise* that day, and are reprinted as Appendix E.
6. Riverside *Enterprise*, April 20, 1950.
7. The Board met during that time in their meeting room in the northeast corner of the courthouse. The room is presently Department X in the Historic Riverside County Courthouse.
8. Upon further analysis, it was found that those who voiced an opinion in some form against the tram outnumbered the proponents by approximately 3:1. Regional Forester Perry Thompson, who chaired the hearing, tallied some statistics about the numbers both for and against, and where they were coming from, for his own edification. He found that:

Location	For the Tramway		Against the Tramway	
	Organizations	Individuals	Organizations	Individuals
Southern Calif.	43	739	64	1409
Northern Calif.	3	29	26	853
Out of State	1	12	30	242
Total:	47	780	120	2504

Davis, August 1973, p. 292.

9. Riverside *Enterprise*, April 20, 21, and 22, 1950; *The Desert Sun*, April 21 and 28, 1950; Davis, August 1973, pp. 273-275.
10. *Ibid.*

11. At this point, there were already discussions and rumors to the effect that only the tramway would be built as a compromise, not all of the other appurtenances originally approved under the Tramway Authority Act.
12. Clark, Lewis F., Richard M. Leonard, and Charlotte E. Mauk. "In Support of the San Jacinto Primitive Area." Unpublished manuscript, April 25, 1950, cited in Davis, August 1973, p. 276.
13. Riverside *Enterprise*, April 20, 21, and 22, 1950; *The Desert Sun*, April 21 and 28, 1950; Davis, August 1973, pp. 275-280.
14. Butcher, Devereux, as quoted in, "Editorial: Dinosaur Monument and Mount San Jacinto." National Parks Magazine, Vol. 24, No. 102, July-September, 1950, p. 112.
15. 16 U.S. Code § 525 - Rights-of-way for wagon roads or railroads, as shown on Cornell Law School's Legal Information Institute (https://www.law.cornell.edu/uscode/text/16/525), accessed June 15, 2022.
16. Unfortunately, multiple attempts to find a copy of this report proved fruitless. National archive branches in Riverside, San Bruno, California, and College Park, Maryland were consulted, as were the Bancroft Library and the Sierra Club library. However, it was available to Richard Carter Davis in the 1960s and 70s, who used it extensively in Chapter 7 of his dissertation. Discussions surrounding the report have therefore been gleaned from Davis' dissertation.
17. Davis, August 1973, pp. 310-311.
18. This is an argument that was used time and again throughout the fight for the tramway. Lots of money and manhours had already been spent on the project, so it could not be denied at this point. While completely unsound logically, it is still used today with many development proposals.
19. *The Desert Sun*, November 10, 1950.
20. *Ibid.*
21. Riverside *Enterprise*, November 7, 1950.
22. *The Desert Sun*, November 10, 1950.
23. Momyer, Joe. "Tram Application Denied." Sierra Club Bulletin, November, 1950, p. 3.
24. While not necessarily documented, members of the Authority did indicate that they had been approached by members of Congress eagerly anticipating the construction of the tramway. Taking the issue to Congress would have really put the entire controversy into the public spotlight, which we have seen is exactly what the Forest Service did not want. Therefore, it was in the best interest of the Forest Service to hammer out a deal.

25. Watts, Lyle F. Letter to the Mt. San Jacinto Winter Park Authority, December 15, 1950, as quoted in Davis, August 1973, pp. 316-317.

26. Riverside *Enterprise*, March 14, 1951.

27. *The Desert Sun*, March 23, 1951.

28. California Legislature, A.B. 3391, 1951 session; An Act to Amend Section 3.3 of the Mount San Jacinto Winter Park Authority Act, Cal. Assembly Bill 3391, Chapter 1004 (Cal. Stat. 1951).

29. Riverside *Enterprise*, May 11, 1951. The opposition was in a tough spot with this legislation. Being in favor of a reduction of the Authority's lands would give almost a tacit approval of the project, while being against it would mean being in favor of a great Authority. While many wanted to restate the general arguments against the tramway (which didn't work), most of the opposition simply waited and prepared for whatever upcoming event would be next.

30. Riverside *Enterprise*, February 27, 1953. Providing public notice was a different entity altogether at that time. Generally, it was not given a lot of publicity at all, mostly just being buried in the legal notice section of a newspaper of "general circulation." In this case, it was published in the Riverside *Enterprise*, but there seems to have been little else done to "get the word out" about this public notice.

31. *The Desert Sun*, April 15, 1954. The 10 subscribers from Palm Springs were: Mrs. Pearl McManus, Harold Hicks (President of the Palm Springs Water Company), Charles Farrell, Culver Nichols, John Williams, Dewey Metzdorf, Earle Strebe, Earl Coffman, Francis Crocker, and Irwin Shuman (owner of the Chi Chi nightclub).

32. *The Desert Sun*, September 3, 1953. The "changed conditions" he refers to would be the end of the Korean War.

33. Riverside *Enterprise*, April 10, 1954.

34. The creation of Jackson Hole National Monument, logging efforts in Olympic National Park, plus proposed dams in Bridge Canyon and others seemed, in the eyes of many Sierra Club members to be much more worthwhile contests than a proposed tramway to Long Valley in the San Jacinto Mountains.

35. Riverside *Enterprise*, April 10, 1954.

36. *The Desert Sun*, April 12, 1954.

37. Riverside *Enterprise*, April 10, 1954.

Chapter 10

Land Exchange Aftermath and Death(?) of the Tramway

When will the Tramway be built? No one seems to know, and the members of the Authority have little to say on this subject except that progress is being made. They will go so far as to say some definite conclusion should be reached this year. Well, if they are not, the chances of ever building the thing are going to be slimmer and slimmer as the years go on . . . A lot of Villagers are already getting pretty skeptical.

Oliver B. Jaynes, Editor of The Desert Sun, *April 25, 1955.*

The battle for the Mt. San Jacinto wilderness still rages, indeed is flaring to new intensity. For more than a decade, this spectacularly beautiful mountain has been the scene of contention between the philosophy of wilderness preservation and the relentless pressures of commercial exploitation

Joe Momyer, "San Jacinto: The Promoter's Nightmare,"
in the Sierra Club Bulletin, January, 1955, pp. 17 – 18.

. . . . the Tramway project . . . would permit complete commercialization of the primitive area. There are enough beer cans and sandwich wrappers beside the trails now without making Round Valley a dump for Palm Springs. Let's really make a resounding stink about this whole proposition.

John Woolfenden, Letter to the Editor,
Idyllwild Town Crier, *May 7, 1954.*

On Monday, April 26, 1954, in the aftermath of the approval of the land exchange, Harry James held a large meeting of conservation groups at his Lolomi Lodge at Lake Fulmor. In attendance were members of his Trailfinders group, along with others from the Sierra Club, Izaac Walton League, American Legion, the Westerners, and the Audubon Society. James tried again to push his idea of allowing only the tramway and terminal facilities, but to no avail. He told the press that opposition to the tramway would continue, and that he was willing to drop the fight against the tramway if the Winter Park Authority Act was amended to restrict development to just the right-of-way and terminal facilities. "The tramway group has said on previous occasions that this is all they want, and I'd like to give them a chance to prove it."[1] He further stated that ski clubs and conservation groups had both surveyed the area and deemed it inadequate for large-scale winter sports development.

Although James swore to continue the fight, the fact was that the opposition to the tramway was hardly in a position to effect any kind of result at this time. The State of California had stated and restated its support for the project through the legislative process, and had also stated its opposition to changing the enacted legislation through that same process. The Federal Government, not wanting to get involved in what they saw as a very local matter, got involved only long enough to ensure a land exchange and no further development in their lands, and left the matter to the locals. Throughout all of these episodes, several things had become clear – the opposition did not have a clear path to enact their goals, were ignorant of the politics of the State of California, and were becoming known more as "nature-boy" obstructionists than anything else. Opposition to the tramway had hit rock bottom, and there was little on the horizon to indicate that their fortunes would change.

However, change they would. By 1954, a new push was emerging to try to stop the tramway project. This new push did not come from the desert, nor one or more of the many conservation groups that had been involved already. This new push came from residents in and around Idyllwild, who speculated that the proposed project, and an influx of thousands of people per day to the mountains, may not only ruin the wilderness areas but may also over commercialize their small town.

At least two of the new opponents of the tramway had their eyes opened during some of the various hearings that had occurred over the past few years. The first, Hunter McConnell, a long-time resident of Idyllwild, had editorialized in the Idyllwild *Town Crier*, that,

> It seems reasonable to conclude that the Tramway is a purely commercial enterprise and with the several thousand people a day that would be required to make it pay, it is hard to un-

derstand how it could remain primitive. . . . I kept thinking how interesting it would be if it were possible to have Teddy Roosevelt here to see what he would do about the proposal to set aside wilderness areas for commercial purposes.[2]

In a similar vein, Richard Elliott, leader of the Desert Sun School in Idyllwild, indicated his change of heart thusly,

> I do not desire the tramway under any circumstances, but have felt it selfish and undemocratic to oppose my wishes to the wishes of a presumed majority. After the hearing, I became doubtful as to the majority of opinion represented.[3]

These two men and others formed the nucleus of a group that began to shift the emphasis of the opposition. The person at the forefront of this new group, though, was Elliott's daughter, Ana Mary, a teacher at the Desert Sun School. She believed that not only should the original Winter Park Authority enabling legislation be overturned, provisions should be made to codify the Mt. San Jacinto area as a wilderness area, to be protected from incursions such as the tramway project.

Several Idyllwild area residents, headed by Ana Mary Elliott, formed the Citizens' Group for the Preservation of the San Jacinto Primitive Area and the Repeal of the Winter Park Authority Act (Citizens' Group) around September, 1954, and began a campaign to get signatures on petitions and begin to effect the repeal of the original Winter Park Authority Act.

> Organized opposition to the proposed San Jacinto tramway has been established in the Idyllwild area with the forming of the [Citizens' Group]. Considerable support throughout southern California has already been promised to this latest effort to remove the threat of commercialization of wilderness areas that would be introduced by the proposed tramway, according to the executive committee of the Citizens Group. Residents may sign petitions opposing the project at Hill business houses.[4]

On November 5, 1954, a Town Hall meeting was held in Idyllwild specifically to address the concerns raised by the newly-formed Citizens' Group. Ana Mary Elliott, as the group's secretary, spoke on many of the issues brought forth. She began by explaining that after a careful study of the original 1945 enabling legislation, many mountain residents believed that construction of the tramway would mean the end of the Mt. San Jacinto Wild Area. She indicated that, in her opinion, the legislation opened up the area for "considerable commercialization of the wilderness" and that it was possible irrespective of statements made by the proponents that they would preserve the natural aspects of the area.[5]

She went on to say that, "the committee feels that in the final analysis the question is whether the Wild Area is to be retained, or is it to become a luxurious resort financed largely by concessions? . . . . We believe that in the long run preservation of the wilderness will be of greater benefit to the people of California."[6]

Other attendees questioned whether the tramway project could supply adequate water to the several hundred thousand visitors expected throughout each year. Elliott mentioned that there were only two major sources of water in the area, and much of that had been spoken for. Both Joe Momyer and Harry James, long-time foes of the tramway, spoke on how they were encouraged by the local efforts to defeat the tramway, since most of what had happened to date had been more on the state and national levels.[7]

Although they seemed a minority, there were also those who spoke in favor of the project. Most of them were from the business community. Therefore, an effort was made by the Citizens' Group to ascertain the feeling of people who either lived or had property in the region. Throughout late 1954 and into 1955, a poll was taken, and the results were overwhelmingly opposed to the tramway – 642 people indicated that they were not in favor of the project, while only 66 supported it.[8]

That poll, and the concerns of many in the mountain area, prompted the Citizen's Group to use it to their advantage. Acting quickly, toward the end of January, they were able to secure and introduce a bill into the California Assembly. AB 3030 was short and to the point – the first section simply sought to repeal the Mount San Jacinto Winter Park Authority Act, and the second sought to "provide for preservation and protection as a natural wilderness area of that portion of the State Park System formerly under the jurisdiction and control of the Mount San Jacinto Winter Park Authority, which por-

WHICH

Do You Want?

You Can't Have Both!

IMPOUNDING THE WATER FOR HUMAN USE AND FLOODING THE AREA WITH PEOPLE WILL DESTROY THE WILDERNESS

•

This series of articles is reprinted (by permission) from the Corona Daily Independent in which they appeared during February, 1955.

Cover of pamphlet published by the Corona Daily Independent outlining the arguments for and against the Palm Springs Aerial Tramway, February 1955 (National Archives).

tion of the State Park System shall be known as the Mount San Jacinto State Wilderness Area."[9]

Several local groups joined the effort of the Citizens' Group to push through AB 3030. These included the board of directors of the Desert Sun School (where Ana Mary Elliott was employed as a teacher), the Regional California State Horsemen's Association, the Idyllwild Arts Foundation, and the San Jacinto Mountain Chapter of the Izaak Walton League. When the legislation hit a snag over the issue of the "Wild Area," it was amended to further explain what was meant and to further enhance the definitions (for the revised text, please see Appendix F).

For a while, it appeared that AB 3030 may have had a chance to succeed. With new blood in the opposition, and the fact that the promoters of the project had now had approval to construct it for ten years with little to show for their efforts, sentiment was growing for the opposition. However, this sentiment was not enough, in the end, to give much credence to the effort. On April 19, 1955, in an effort to try to get the Riverside County Board of Supervisors on board with the opposition, Harry James and others appeared before the Board to get them to adopt a resolution supporting AB 3030. Arguing against it was Francis Crocker and V. W. Grubbs of the Winter Park Authority Board. The Board of Supervisors were wholeheartedly unconvinced and four of the five supervisors voted down the proposal to support the assembly bill. Only Roman Warren voted in favor, stating not that he was against the tram, but that the arguments of the opposition should at least be given a bit more study before the Board acted.[10]

Undaunted, Joe Momyer decided to try another tactic only a week later. He and others appeared before the Board, asking them to support a compromise wherein the lands over which the Authority would have jurisdiction would be limited to those needed for the tramway itself plus the two stations and parking lot – in effect the compromise that had been mentioned and championed by Harry James for some time. Reluctantly, on April 26, 1955, the Board agreed to hear the case put forth by Momyer and others.

The arguments heard on April 26 went about as far as those heard the week before. Proponents argued that this was simply another delaying tactic by the opposition – one that would require reapplying for all permits due to the reduced land size. The Board agreed, indicating that their approval of such a measure would be "muddying" the situation so far into the process. Earl Coffman, longtime proponent of the tramway, sent a telegram from Sacramento where he was to fight the AB 3030 effort. He indicated that there was "no possible basis for compromise" in this proposal. To be economically viable, there had to be the ability to develop facilities in the mountain region. Harry Lockwood, attorney for the Authority, put it more bluntly – "There will be no compromise. Absolutely no."[11]

The next day saw the AB 3030 heard in the Assembly in Sacramento. The same arguments were put forth, and it was agreed in general that too much had been done and spent to date to simply pull the project at this point. That said, an ominous sign was given to the proponents of the tramway project. One Assemblyman, Vernon Kilpatrick, who had aided Harry James years before, wrote to James and indicated that, "I think [the] Mt. San Jacinto cableway people went away with a pretty good conclusion that they had better do something within the next two years or be prepared to forfeit their rights to the Mt. San Jacinto State Park."[12] It seems as though several people were becoming impatient with the effort to construct the tramway – still, AB 3030 was dead within a few days.

Over the next six months, little occurred. Several members of the opposition made public statements to the effect that they would continue the fight against the tramway, but in reality, little was done. That's not to say that encouragement was not on the horizon – it was, this time from the State Legislature.

For a number of reasons, in 1957, the State Legislature of California opted to study the need for a comprehensive park and recreation program. During the fall of that year, the Subcommittee on Beaches and Parks was formed as a subcommittee of the Assembly Interim Committee on Conservation, Planning, and Public Works. As part of their charge, the Subcommittee on Beaches and Parks opted to visit the San Jacinto Mountains, study the arguments regarding its preservation being presented, and try to ascertain how it could be folded into the comprehensive study.[13] As part of their survey, they planned to visit the upper reaches of the San Jacinto Mountains, and Ana Mary Elliott was more than happy to meet with the legislative subcommittee to discuss her arguments and aid in their tour.

On October 24, three legislators, Tom Erwin of Whittier, Eugene Nisbet of Upland, and Jesse Unruh of Los Angeles, began a horseback tour of the high country, including Long and Round Valleys, and the proposed site of the mountain station. The next day, the group met with Palm Springs backers of the tram to get their side of things. At the ensuing hearing, Assemblyman Tom Erwin had some very blunt words for the tramway backers regarding what the legislators perceived to be the well-organized lobby fighting the proposal:

> It's never settled and it never will be settled until it's built. The conservation groups are very powerful and they will continue to come before the Legislature. It's just one of the things we have in our democracy. . . . . In the years to come, we're going to have repeal legislation – there isn't any question about it.[14]

It is obvious that tempers were beginning to flare at this point. With all that both sides had been through, with little to no chance for any compromise, it was only a matter of time before this would happen. Proponents of the project indicated that continued opposition to the project might jeopardize their ability to sell bonds, and hence may be endangering the project. Some of the subcommittee members were not phased, and in fact openly questioned whether the State Parks Commission was actually in favor of the project, or just felt coerced by the original enabling legislation. Henry Lockwood, the Authority's attorney, fired off a quick response: "They were not coerced in any manner. This is simply a repetition of falsehoods to the point where the people who made them believe them themselves!" Eugene Nisbet responded to Lockwood, saying that "I think they're just as sincere in their opposition as you are in your promotion."[15]

Nisbet concluded the hearing by asking Lockwood what facilities were being planned in the mountains. Lockwood indicated that only the mountain terminal, with a snack bar, restaurant, ski shop, and living quarters for tramway employees. He stated that there would be no hotel, as the opponents had feared.[16]

As an interesting aside, the trip to the San Jacinto Mountains by members of the Legislative subcommittee did result in new proposals for discussing and permitting uses within State Parks. When the final report was issued in March, 1957, it indicated that one factor that should be used in determining whether to open an area to additional use should be a "capacity survey" which would take into count the condition of soils, flora, and fauna, and the effects that introducing many people into the environment would have (for the discussion of the subcommittee's findings, please see Appendix H).

The remainder of 1955 and most of 1956 were filled with a few minor attempts at trying to reverse the construction of the tramway. These paled, though, in light of what most of the opposition saw as thc next, biggest, and best opportunity kill the proposal once and for all, namely, the renewal of the State Park Commission approval.

Back in 1951, the State Parks Commission had granted a five-year extension to the agreement with the Winter Park Authority, originally approved in 1947. This agreement, it will be remembered, granted access to the tramway across California State Park lands – an absolute necessity for the project. It also allowed for the tram itself and appurtenant uses, per the original enabling legislation. In 1951, the Authority asked for a ten-year extension, knowing that several hurdles still remained. The Parks Commission, though, settled on a five-year extension with the provision that the Authority would have to sell at least $1,000,000 in bonds by the end of the term to keep the agreement active. Needless to say, the Authority had not sold any bonds, let alone $1,000,000 worth, and so in December, 1956, they had to return to the Commission to request a further extension.

This need for a further extension must have been on the calendar of every opposition group to the tramway, for when the hearing was held on December 21, 1956, they were more than ready. As we've already seen, the original Parks Commission members viewed the language in the enabling legislation as a mandate to enter into an agreement with the Authority. During the hearing, Edward W. Cunningham, the legal counsel for the Sierra Club, forcefully argued that most of the time, the legislation used the word "may" instead of "shall," thereby making any agreement between the two bodies discretionary, not mandatory. He further argued that even though the Authority was always referred to as a "State" agency, the fact that a majority of its members came from either Palm Springs or Riverside County made this point moot – it was a local agency with local interests only. Thus, a renewal of the agreement would be giving local control to State property.

This time, those arguments stuck. In addition, opposition members had had more than ten years to make their point, and members of the Commission (and in fact, most people who had been following the project), had a hard time denying the fact that after more than ten years, nothing had been accomplished on the tramway except for several surveys and many more engineering and geotechnical studies.

Joseph Knowland of Oakland, a member of the Commission and a staunch supporter of the tramway from the beginning, even could not deny the reality of the lack of progress on the project. During the hearing, he indicated that the Authority had been given every opportunity to finance the project and had failed. Now, as 1956 was turning to 1957, there was even less opportunity in his mind to secure the needed financing due to a bad bond market.[17]

Having heard all of the testimony, including the statements made by Cunningham, Commissioner Charles Kasch indicated that in his view,

> This Commission has complied with the legislation and exercised due diligence in entering the agreement and any of the powers granted to the Park Commission [to contract with the Authority] are not mandatory but discretionary. . . . . The responsibility of the Park Commission has been fully met and it is at an end.[18]

With this statement, the California State Parks Commission voted unanimously to deny the Mt. San Jacinto Winter Park Authority's application for extension. The tramway project was effectively dead.

Reactions to the apparent death of the long wished-for and spoken-about tramway were swift. Oliver Jaynes, the consummate backer of the tramway and editor of *The Desert Sun*, penned an editorial entitled, "Someone Should at Least Say Thanks!" In it, he stated,

> The Tramway is dead--long live the Tramway!
>
> Without even a memorial service—or a gathering of mourners—Mt. San Jacinto Aerial Tramway was laid quietly to rest last week. Scarred, bruised, and enfeebled by bad luck and pesky foes the "great idea" was given the coup de grace by the California State Park Board. Failure of the Park Board to renew a contract with the Tramway Authority to permit use of land in San Jacinto State Park for Tramway purposes was the death blow. Only formality now remaining is for the State Legislature to sign the death certificate.[19]

Chapter 10 Endnotes

1. Riverside *Enterprise*, April 27, 1954.
2. Idyllwild *Town Crier*, April 29, 1950.
3. Elliott, Richard, letter to Regional Forester Perry A. Thompson, April 27, 1950, in Davis, August 1973, p. 356. The hearing referred to was the April 20, 1950 hearing regarding a right-of-way over USFS property.
4. Idyllwild *Town Crier*, October 8, 1954.
5. Riverside *Press*, November 9, 1954.
6. *Ibid.*
7. *Ibid.*
8. Riverside *Press*, January 15, 1955. To be fair, support for the tramway increased outside of the mountain region of Riverside County.
9. California Legislature, A. B. 3030, 61st session (1955).
10. Riverside *Enterprise*, April 19, 1955. For a series of editorials in the Riverside *Press* concerning the fight to have the Board of Supervisors weigh in on the matter, please see Appendix G.
11. Riverside *Enterprise*, April 26, 1955.
12. Kilpatrick, Vernon, to Harry James, May 2, 1955, as quoted in Davis, August 1973, p. 375.
13. California Legislature, Assembly, Interim Committee on Conservation, Planning, and Public Works. "A State-Wide Park and Recreation Program. Report of the Subcommittee on Beaches and Parks, a Subcommittee of the Assembly Interim Committee on Conservation Planning and Public Works, Assembly Interim Committee reports, 1955-57, XIII, No. 12 (March, 1957).
14. Riverside *Enterprise*, April 26, 1955.
15. *Ibid.*
16. *Ibid.* This is an age-old concern and trick in the constant battle between environmentalists and developers. Things are promised in hearings, not codified in law, and then can rear their heads later on. The opponents of the tramway were quite keen to this, stating that while the present Authority members may indicate that no hotel or other facilities would be constructed, that is not to say that future members would take that same position, especially if the enabling legislation was still in place to allow them to.
17. *The Desert Sun*, December 21, 1956.
18. California State Park Commission minutes, December 21, 1956, as quoted in Davis, August 1973, p. 386.
19. Jaynes, Oliver. "Someone Should at Least Say Thanks!" *The Desert Sun*, December 27, 1956. The entire editorial by Jaynes is reproduced as Appendix I.

Chapter 11

The Tramway Rises from the Ashes

We believe that the right thing to do is to hold Mt. San Jacinto State Park as it is for the next generation. If they wish to convert it into a luxurious resort that's their decision to make.

Editorial, Idyllwild Town Crier, *January 8, 1960.*

[The Tramway] will provide a heretofore inaccessible park for all to enjoy, instead of a few goats and fresh air beatniks!

Thomas Wolfe (President of the Desert Ranch Owners Association), Riverside Enterprise, *December 19, 1959.*

Many people saw the refusal of the State Park Commission to renew their approval of the tramway project as a death knell. While still believing in the worthiness of the tramway, most people understood that the project had run its course and that since little had been done construction wise, there stood little chance of it ever actually getting off the ground.

One such entity that steadfastly refused to believe this was the Idyllwild-based Citizens Group. Sure, in the mind of the Citizens Group, the project had suffered a major setback, but the legislation allowing it was still in effect, and therefore constructing a tramway was still a distinct possibility. In addition, many in the group could not believe that after so many years of working so closely with state legislators, high-ranking trade officials, and other powerful people that the proponents of the tramway did not still have some tricks up their sleeves that they could play.

As 1957 began, and with it another session of the State Legislature, the Citizens Group stood ready with yet another bill to repeal the original enabling legislation for the tramway project. Sure, this tactic had been tried on several previous occasions with no effect, but this time, it was reasoned, would be different and this time would be the best opportunity to finally kill the project once and for all.

The 1957 attempt to kill the tramway was in the form of Assembly Bill 1361, dated January 18, 1957. Unlike previous attempts, though, this one had eight sponsors from various locations throughout Southern California, which gives some indication that there was much more support for the opposition at that time.[1]

Harry James, for his part, was left out of the planning of this repeal bill, but still argued for a "tram only" compromise that would allow just the tram and its stations to be built, but not allowing any of the other myriad of items listed in the enabling legislation. As can be imagined, this so-called compromise was not part of the vocabulary of the Winter Park Authority, that saw building just the tram and no other improvements as economic folly.[2]

On April 10, 1957, AB 1361 was heard before the Conservation, Planning and Public Works Committee of the Assembly. Riverside County Assemblyman Leland M. Backstrand led the opposition to the bill, and was bolstered by State Senator Nelson Dilworth. Testimony was heard on both sides, apparently neither of which brought up any new points. In the end, the bill was defeated by a vote of 12 – 9. Once again, the opponents of the tram had failed in the legislature.[3]

Putting the efforts for and against AB 1361 aside, the period between the "death knell" vote of the California State Parks Commission in December, 1956 and late 1959 was marked by a perceived opinion that the tramway was no more. However, there was lots of behind-the-scenes action on the part of the tramway proponents to keep the project from totally collapsing. In looking at the 1956 denial of a new contract, one of the major factors in the Authority's inability to halt or at least delay the contract's termination was financial. It will be remembered that all of the monies that would go to the numerous studies and construction of the project had to come from the sale of bonds. In 1956, as in so many years during that era, the bond market was in a less-than-desirable state. Overall average interest rates had remained high, which resulted in an unfavorable market for the potential sale of nearly $15 million in bonds in the mid-1950s, which at that time was the estimated cost of the project.

By the fall of 1959, though, two things had come about to greatly improve the financial outlook for the tram. One was a marked reduction in interest rates, with a corresponding improvement in the bond market. As with all economic trends, markets go up and they come down, and by late 1959, they were in a very favorable position to allow for the sale of bonds. The second item to improve the chances for the tramway was a re-engineering of the project itself, substantially lowering the cost.

Palm Springs in the 1950s (Author's collection).

Throughout the "silent" period of 1957-1959, engineers worked to firm up the actual construction documents and studies needed for the project. By the fall of 1959, with better materials and more information, they were confident that they could make a straight run up the mountain with no intermediary stop as had been the proposal all along. That is, the tram could be constructed so that riders would only go through the valley and mountain stations with no third station in the middle.[4] This drastically cut projected construction costs so that by the fall of 1959, the Authority was looking at a requirement of $7,700,000, or about half of what had been anticipated just three years before.[5]

With all of these new factors, in November, 1959, Henry Lockwood, legal counsel for the Authority, appeared before the California State Park Commission at its meeting in Santa Barbara to say that the proponents of the tramway were in a position to ask the Commission to reinstate the previous agreement that had expired.[6] Stating that the original enabling legislation from 1945 had been a mandate for the Commission to enter into such an agreement, the Commission ordered staff to investigate the issue and come back with recommendations at the December meeting. It further set January 15, 1960, as a date for a public hearing on the matter. The opposition to the tram, which by now had moved on to other issues and was caught rather off-guard, did mount a presence at the hearings. The *Desert Sun* summed up the feelings thusly,

> The battle over the proposed tramway on Mt. San Jacinto was renewed yesterday, with representatives of four Southern California conservation and outdoor groups opposing a request of the Winter Park Authority for a five-year renewal of its contract.[7]

The long break in any action on the tramway had led many of the "old guard" opposition to be indisposed by late 1959-1960. Ana Mary Elliott was in Vienna studying music, some of the legal counsel for the Sierra Club had parted ways with that group, and Harry James had only sent a representative to the November hearing.

At the November hearing, James' representative asked that the tramway simply be removed from any further consideration (i.e. terminate the issue). Obviously that wasn't going to happen and that idea was quickly removed from discussion. It is at this point that a new tactic was brought to bear by the opposition. If the tramway cannot simply be overturned, they asked, then it should be made to operate in such a way as to not exceed the carrying capacity of the wilderness area into which it would encroach.[8]

This was a bold new tactic undertaken by the opposition – a tactic that had been given to them early in 1957 by the State Legislature but without an opportunity to invoke it until now. It relied on the concept of a "carrying capacity," the idea of which had been around since at least the 1930s. At that time, National Park Service biologist E. Lowell Sumner pondered "how large a crowd can be turned loose in a wilderness without destroying its essential qualities."[9] He went on to conclude that recreational use of an area should be kept "within the carrying capacity."[10]

The concept of a carrying capacity as it related to the San Jacinto Mountains and the proposed tramway had come up in 1957 when the State Legislature of California opted to study the need for a comprehensive park and recreation program (see Chapter 10). At that time, what concerned the subcommittee that was formed as part of this study was not construction of the tram itself but the effect that putting thousands of people into the wilderness area would have on the natural environment. This too was a burgeoning study area and not much had been done about it up to this time. After the subcommittee studied what it needed, it concluded in its final report that it was,

O. Earl Coffman (left) and Francis Crocker enjoy a minute of levity in 1954. They saw the Palm Springs Aerial Tramway from start to finish (James Landells photo).

> impressed by the critical condition of the San Jacinto Park and wilderness area even with its present limited use. It believes that any more intensive use of this area should be based on the capacity of the area determined by sound conservation principles. The scientific determination of the best use of an area, relating to the conditions of the watershed and the preservation of the area itself appear appropriate criteria for deciding the relative intensity of use and should be one of the tools available to the Division of Recreation and Beaches and Parks in their planning process.[11]

At the same time, Ana Mary Elliott was interested in pursuing the possibility of studying the carrying capacity of the region and contacted members of the faculty of the Natural Resources Department at Long Beach State College. Through various connections, she and others were able to effect a fellowship to have a graduate student study the effects of human use of the San Jacinto Mountains.

The result of this fellowship was a report entitled *A Study of the Human Use of the Mount San Jacinto Wild Area in the San Jacinto Mountain Range and the Surrounding San Bernardino National Forest Area* by DeBoyd Smith. Smith's study concluded that the San Jacinto Wilderness Area was seeing increased usage, what parks and campgrounds there were were being overrun, and the region was in danger of losing the wilderness for which it was known. As part of his findings, he concluded,

> . . . . In view of the present natural conditions of the San Jacinto State Park Primitive Area, and the use to which it is exposed, it would seem that a greatly expanded usage could not be tolerated.
> . . . . An influx [of people] with little or no training in forestry practices or conservation education, would soon obliterate the scenic wilderness as it exists today.
> . . . . There are many examples of the overuse of mountain resort areas, national parks, and other public camp areas throughout the State of California and throughout the nation. In view of the intent and purposes of the establishment of the San Jacinto State Park, as well as the accepted pattern of its present use, it seems proper to continue the plea for repeal of the Winter Park Authority.[12]

With all of this aforementioned information and the recommendations of the subcommittee, in 1957, the State Legislature passed legislation requiring that "before any park or recreation area developmental plan is made, the Director of Natural Resources shall cause to be made a land carrying capacity survey of the proposed park or recreational area, including in such survey such factors as soil, moisture, and natural cover."[13]

Therefore, at the November, 1959 meeting of the California State Parks Commission, when Harry James' Trailfinder representative indicated that the tramway should be made to work within the carrying capacity of the wilderness area, he had recently-enacted legislation to back him up. As part of the staff report and recommendations, there would be a carrying capacity report.

When the report was issued at the December meeting, it consisted of just two pages, but made a damning prediction for the tramway supporters. Its conclusion was that, "the capacity of the wild area as such for the tramway project is zero; as soon as the tramway is built, the wilderness will be gone, and with it the State's understanding with the Forest Service."[14]

Neither that statement nor the additional statements made by the opposition had any influence on the State Parks Commission at its hearing of January 15, 1960. That hearing saw many of the same arguments used on both sides, plus the addition of the carrying capacity argument, but to no avail. Still believing that the original 1945 enabling legislation made it a mandate for the State to enter into an agreement for the tram with the Winter Park Authority, the Commission voted unanimously to recommend that the Department of Natural Resources renegotiate an agreement with the Authority.[15] The Mount San Jacinto Winter Park Authority and the Palm Springs Aerial Tramway were back in business.

Ernest Gray postcard view of
Idyllwild in Winter (Author's collection).

Chapter 11 Endnotes

1. *The Desert Sun*, January 29, 1957. The eight sponsors wcrc: Ernest R. Geddes of Claremont, James L. Holms of Santa Barbara, W. S. (Bill) Grant of Long Beach, Frank G. Bonelli of Huntington Park, M. A. Burke of Alhambra, George G. Crawford of San Diego, L. D. House of Brawley, and A. I. Stewart of Pasadena.
2. Davis, August 1973, p. 389.
3. Riverside *Enterprise*, April 10, 1957.
4. This third station had been part of the plan since the initial concepts of the aerial tramway.
5. Davis, August 1973, pp. 405-407. Removing the center station meant no grading and construction of that station, no additional cars, and no additional mechanical needs associated with three stations and two tramways.
6. This was by no means a new statement. Proponents of the Tramway had been stating publicly that the State Parks Board would entertain a reapplication for the Tramway should the financial outlook and their ability to sell bonds improve. "Coffman recently reported that the park board has indicated it would consider renewing the authority's contract when and if the authority can obtain financing for the project. The tramway was held up for many years by difficulties in acquiring rights of way. After finally clearing the path and getting authority to issue bonds, the tramway ran into the current "tight money" situation and scarcity of investors" (Riverside *Enterprise*, April 11, 1957).
7. *The Desert Sun*, November 21, 1959.
8. Davis, August 1973, p. 408.
9. Sumner, 1936, p. 58.
10. *Ibid.*
11. California Legislature, Assembly, Interim Committee on Conservation, Planning, and Public Works, A State-Wide Park and Recreation Program. Report of the Subcommittee on Beaches and Parks, a Subcommittee of the Assembly Interim Committee on Conservation Planning and Public Works, Assembly Interim Committee reports, 1955-57, XII, No. 12 (March, 1957), pp. 61 - 62.
12. Smith, 1957, pp. 172-173. The author is indebted to Mark Smith, grandson of DeBoyd Smith, for taking the time to locate and furnish a copy of his grandfather's work to me.
13. Davis, August 1973, pp. 381-382.

14. State of California, Division of Beaches and Parks. "Mount San Jacinto State Park, Load Carrying Capacity," December 9, 1959, as quoted in Davis, August 1973, p. 409. In addition, the Idyllwild *Town Crier* came out with a forceful editorial going point by point against the tram and the implications of such a project on future generations. That editorial, dated January 8, 1960, just a week before the hearing, is reproduced as Appendix J.

15. There was a slightly different situation in California politics at this time. In 1959, the Legislature had enacted a new law that essentially stripped the Parks Commission of its ability to actually make agreements. In effect, it made the Commission a policy body with the ability to recommend to the Department of Natural Resources that it enter into an agreement. Therefore, any new contract with the Winter Park Authority would have to be negotiated with the Department of Natural Resources upon the recommendation of the California State Parks Commission. This added another step in the process, but that was about all.

Chapter 12

The Opposition Isn't Done

If they have not wrecked [the Tramway project] *beyond repair, the band of narrow-minded conservationists will discover it more difficult now to find people in sympathy with their arguments against the long sought project.*

Editorial, The Desert Sun, *April 20, 1960*[1]

There is a place for resorts, but conservationists believe that the San Jacinto Wild Area should not be sacrificed to commercialism. In time, these wild lands can prove to be of greater value to the country than another resort.

Ernie Maxwell, editorial in Pacific Discovery Magazine, *January-February, 1955*

Just as the January 15, 1960 meeting of the California State Parks Commission signaled the rebirth of the Palm Springs Aerial Tramway, it also signaled another rebirth of the opposition to it. By 1960, many people in California, from lay person to State Representative, had become what we of today would consider more "environmentally aware." Years of hearing about wilderness, carrying capacity, conservation, and preservation had had some effect, and the zeitgeist present in 1960 when the Authority received a second chance was vastly different than when it got its first approval back in 1948.[2] Therefore, despite a favorable review by the Parks Commission (and subsequent favorable recommendation), there were new people in many positions who sought either to defeat the tramway or somehow curtail its ability to effectively operate.

The next challenge to the proponents of the tramway was to secure an agreement with the Department of Natural Resources. Negotiations for that agreement were expected to take about two weeks, but in the end, they dragged out for more than six months. At this time, opponents of the Tramway turned their attention to urging that every effort be made to restrict developments, thereby attempting to lessen the Tramway's impact and viability. Harry James, who had advocated for such a course early on, indicated that if a "tram only" plan was carried out successfully, the project could result in no serious threat to the wilderness area.[3]

Harry James in his younger days (Special Collections & University Archives, UCR Library).

The proponents needed to begin negotiations with the Department of Natural Resources immediately. Opponents used this time to try to work with State officials themselves. Their goal was to place into the contract a number of ideas they had that could lessen or delay the impact of the Tramway.

Just a few days after the approval was secured on January 15, Nathan Clark, a long-standing and well-respected Sierra Club leader, suggested to Edward Dolder and Charles DeTurk, the chiefs of the Division of Beaches and Parks of the Department of Natural Resources (Dolder was leaving and DeTurk was taking his place) that the entire contract be reviewed for approval by an "advisory committee" of five conservationist organizations, all of which had opposed the tramway. Dolder and DeTurk liked this idea and a group was established, including Nathan Clark (Sierra Club), Ralph Rutledge (The Nature Conservancy), Ernie Maxwell (the editor of the Idyllwild *Town Crier*, representing the Izaak Walton League), Art Johnson (Federation of Outdoor Clubs), and Harry James (Desert Protective Council).[4]

In essence, this group and the rest of the opposition hoped to put enough restrictions in the contract that sale of bonds for the project would be extremely difficult if not impossible. Unfortunately, many of the plans that would arise over the next few months reached the ears of Governor Edmund G. Brown, who indicated that he was tired of delays and forbid them to include any provisions in the contract meant to hinder the bond sales in any way.[5]

One of the attempted tactics was brought up by Ralph Rutledge, a retired professor who headed the Southern California Chapter of the Nature Conservancy. He asked that the plan of development be reviewed by medical personnel of the Department of Public Health. His reasoning? The proposed descent of the Tramway was, in his opinion, too steep and too quick. People could become subjected to fainting spells, headaches, and other issues related to a rapid descent from a relatively high altitude. In proposing this, Rutledge was trying to elongate the riding time of each tram ride, thereby cutting the number of rides available per day with a subsequent loss of revenue. This was quickly excused as bad science.

Another approach was posited by Sierra Club members Nathan Clark and Clark Jones, together with Art Johnson, the President of the Federation of Western Outdoor Clubs. Together, they joined forces with Rutledge and others to advance a position whereby the entire contract would be subject to review by the California District Securities Commission prior to any approval.

This approach, and several others, were bantered about by various groups and individuals for a while, along with the aforementioned advisory committee. By the beginning of July, it was learned that the ad hoc advisory committee would be able to take their list of ideas/requests and present them to Edward Dolder in a meeting with him on July 12. Therefore, the committee boiled down the list to a total of six requests, which were as follows:

1. A request to amend the clause in the contract protecting natural features. It should be made more specific by referring to "flora, fauna, and other" features;
2. A request to strengthen the section detailing accommodations for employees to include only those "essential for the maintenance and protection of the area;"
3. A request for specific insurance requirements;
4. A request for a bond to be purchased by the Authority to ensure that all structures would be removed and the sites regraded if the Tramway should close;
5. A request to delete a clause which forbid any amendment without approval of the bondholders;
6. A request to require approval of the Authority's bonds by the California District Securities Commission prior to sale.[6]

Harry Wendelken postcard view of deer in the San Jacinto Mountains (Author's collection).

The July 12 meeting had mixed results for both sides. Despite having apparent sympathies for several of these recommendations, Dolder only forwarded the first two requests, which were ultimately placed into the final agreement. Requests 3, 4, and 5 had to do with the sale of bonds, which was off limits so far as the Governor was concerned. The last request was out of the hands of the Division of Beaches and Parks chief.[7]

With just two weeks to go before the meeting of the State Parks Board, not much else could be done. However, by now, most people were as satisfied as they could be. "Conservationists Agree on Proposal" is how the Riverside *Enterprise* headlined the news, and in effect, they had agreed on it.[8] To them and others, it was obvious that the tram was going to be approved and constructed – it was a matter of just how much could be exacted from the project in guarantees, both from a conservation standpoint and from a viability standpoint.

The State Parks Board recommended approval at their July 22 meeting, which meant that the agreement could move forward to the Director of the Department of Natural Resources for final approval. That approval came on August 4, 1960, when DeWitt Nelson, director of the Department of Natural Resources, signed the new, 5-year agreement.[9] A triumphant editorial in *The Desert Sun* congratulated many,

> Plans for the Mt. San Jacinto Tramway are proceeding again with the signing of a new contract with the state. Things are really looking up and when it is finished the populace will be looking up, too, and riding up. Much credit goes to two Villagers who never gave up.
>
> Earl Coffman and Francis Crocker, members of the Tram Authority never threw up their hands in despair despite what appeared to be a never-ending parade of obstacles.
>
> They kept that goal of the giant airlift to the upper mountains in mind despite opposition from nature lovers who didn't want that area opened for all to enjoy, a World War, steel strikes, a weak bond market and the like.
>
> Ever since Frank Crocker stood on Palm Canyon Drive on a hot day in August, just about 23 years ago today, and remarked to a friend, Carl Barkow of The Sun, how nice it would be if there were a quick way of getting up that mountain side to the cool top, the fight to top all hurdles and make the tramway a reality has been under way.[10]

The agreement adopted by the Department of Natural Resources did take into consideration some of the concerns of the opposition, but certainly not all. While it did grant powers to the Authority to use State lands for the purposes of constructing and operating an aerial tramway, it did so within a much smaller area than originally granted. Now, under the new agreement, the Authority would be able to operate on only four sections of land instead of the dozens afforded it previously.[11] Furthermore, in a big win for the conservationists, it severely limited what the Authority could do within the wilderness area. It will be remembered that the original language of the 1945 enabling legislation stated,

> The authority may acquire, construct or complete roads, highways, trams, tramways, aerial cableways, up-skis, ski-lifts, parking areas, skiing areas, areas for tobogganing, coasting, snowshoeing, sledding, ice skating, ski huts, hotels, pensions, lodges, restaurants, buses, buildings, and all other works, properties and structures necessary, convenient or useful for the development of winter sports, and any other

Map showing the final area of influence of the Mt. San Jacinto Winter Park Authority per the 1960 agreement (Google Earth Maps).

recreational facilities within the territorial limits of the authority . . . It may also acquire or construct and operate and maintain water supplies, and power and drainage systems, necessary, convenient, or useful to the project purposes of the authority . . .

Under the new agreement, only the following was allowed,

> Trails, pedestrian paths, portable rope tows, skiing areas, areas for tobogganing, coasting, snowshoeing, sledding, ice-skating rink, warming huts for employees and visitors, a restaurant, housing for employees essential for maintenance and protection of the area, a gift shop, a first aid station, and a ranger station.[12]

In a major defeat, though, for the conservationists, the new agreement did not include any provisions for remediation of the area should the tramway fail and have to be removed. This was seen as a particular problem, since many people had doubts as to the viability of the project.[13]

With the director's signature on the agreement, the Palm Springs Aerial Tramway was officially resurrected and well on its way to becoming reality. Nothing stood in its way now, but the sale of bonds and actual construction would still be several months off. From this point forward, the opposition no longer existed in any tangible form. Sure, people were still upset about the prospect of the mountainside being marred by construction, and even more concerned about a great deal of construction taking place, only to discover that the project was not possible, was too expensive, or the principals unable to complete what they needed to. As we know today, none of those scenarios took place. But in 1960, all the opposition could do now was hope for the best.

Chapter 12 Endnotes

1. This editorial, entitled "Attitudes Have Changed," is reprinted as Appendix K.
2. We're speaking here of State approval at the Parks Commission level.
3. Davis, August 1973, p. 412.
4. *Ibid*, p. 414. Harry James was working with and on behalf of the Desert Protective Council at this time pushing their idea of a massive nature reserve to encompass much of the San Jacinto and Santa Rosa Mountains. It appears that nothing came of this, but at the time it was quite controversial, invoking the ire of sports groups and Chambers of Commerce alike.
5. *Ibid*, p. 412. Because of this, Art Johnson wrote to Harry James that "Brown has taken the attitude that the Winter Park Authority is a State agency. . . . . Palm Springs has gotten to him. They have wined and dined him." This statement brings up an interesting factoid about how the Tramway stayed at the forefront for as long as it did. In conversations with Kitty Kieley, granddaughter of O. Earl Coffman, she stressed that her grandfather knew most if not all of the main players in this episode, especially at the State level. Well positioned to "wine and dine" people, Coffman, the owner and operator of arguably Palm Springs' most famous resort, the Desert Inn, had the means and wherewithal to effect this kind of back-stage lobbying, and did (Kieley, Personal communication with the author, March 23, 2023).
6. Davis, August 1973, pp. 415-416.
7. *Ibid.*
8. Riverside *Enterprise*, July 15, 1960.
9. Riverside *Enterprise*, August 6, 1960.
10. "This Side of the Sun" by Phat, editorial in *The Desert Sun*, August 10, 1960.
11. Idyllwild *Town Crier*, July 15, 1960. The Authority's area of influence now stood at just Sections 13, 14, 23, and 24 of T4S, R3E, with major construction being allowed only within Section 23.
12. State of California, "Agreement" (AG-7/18/1960), August 4, 1960.
13. Idyllwild *Town Crier*, July 15, 1960.

Chapter 13

On With The Tram

I asked Earl (Coffman) to pinch me. It didn't seem possible that it could be true.

Francis Crocker to The Desert Sun, *July 7, 1961, upon successful sale of the Tramway revenue bonds.*

Crusades sacrifice other values.

Ana Mary Elliott to Richard Carter Davis, August, 1970, when asked if she would do it all again.[1]

With the completion of the agreement of August 4, 1960, final preparations could be made. Construction plans and specifications based on the two-station system had to be finalized, and a new economic feasibility report had to be prepared based upon the limitations placed on the Authority by the new agreement. Little time was wasted in getting these items started.

In late September, 1960, meetings were held in Palm Springs relative to the economic feasibility report. More trips were made to Chino Canyon and the Long Valley area to ascertain the latest engineering data. O. Earl Coffman, the chair of the Authority, came out to assure local residents that these meetings "do not mean that the Tramway will be constructed tomorrow, but merely indicate that work is being done to set the scene for the sale of revenue bonds in the very near future." Coffman addressed the setbacks of the past 20 years, stating that,

> Although we were pretty upset over the setbacks we were faced with on the Tramway during the past score of years, today we are not just being optimistic when we say that the project is going ahead. . . . . The delay has been much in our favor because many companies have come up with new developments in installation and equipment, and many companies have made a full-time job out of building tramways.[2]

It took nearly a year to compile data, perform studies, finish the plans and specs, and get everything ready for the next step in the process – the sale of bonds. For years, the Authority had been trying to do just that – sell its bonds, generate some income, and of course, fund construction of the tramway. Now, that was becoming a reality.

For the economic information, the Authority once again turned to Coverdale and Colpitts, Consulting Engineers from New York. They had been with the Authority almost from the beginning, so it was merely a matter of updating some of the assumptions of previous reports in order to finalize theirs.

Once Coverdale and Colpitts had completed their work, the final amount to be collected in bond sales was set at $7.7 million.[3] This would cover construction of all facilities, initial operating costs, purchase of land for the Valley Station, and nearly 20 years' worth of past legal fees, consulting engineers' fees, reports, studies, travel expenses, and various other expenses that had been borne by many individuals seeking to have the proposed tramway approved. In rough amounts, some of the costs included construction costs of $4.8 million, bond negotiating and selling costs of nearly $2 million, and fees to Henry Lockwood (legal counsel to the Authority) of $100,000.

In determining potential revenue, Coverdale and Colpitts rather optimistically determined that the Authority's annual revenue for bond debt service would be nearly $1.4 million, which was calculated by assuming $630,000 in operating expenses and revenue of just over $2 million, based on a charge of $4 per person to ride the tram. Furthermore, they estimated that 40% of the ridership would occur in the months of January, February, and March, while the other 60% would occur over the rest of the year.

By June, 1961, Earl Coffman announced that the bonds would go on sale, but that no construction could or would start until all of the bonds were sold - "the deal must wait until all the bonds are sold. You can't build half a tramway!"[4] There was talk of some potential offers, but in the end, the entire set of bonds was purchased by the firm of Bear, Stearns, and Company for $7.7 million, minus 5.25%, or $404,250. In speaking of the sale later, it was long-time Authority board member V. W. Grubbs' opinion that there would have been no bids at a public sale, and so selling to Bear Stearns was their only option.[5] Whether that was true or not was immaterial at the time. What did matter was that the Authority had all of the cash needed to begin construction right away.

When exactly construction began is hard to nail down. During the week of June 5, 1961, a contract was signed between the Authority and L. C. Dixon of Alhambra for construction of the Tramway.[6] July 7, 1961, is generally given as the start of construction, as that was the date that the revenue bonds were officially sold. However, as reported in *The Desert Sun*, on that date, there were already survey crews at work for the main contractor, L. C. Dixon of Alhambra, California. Whatever the start date, the agreement called for a construction period of 660 days, or 22 months.[7]

Helicopter flying materials to construction sites for the Palm Springs Aerial Tramway (Palm Springs Aerial Tramway photo).

Construction of the Palm Springs Aerial Tramway lasted the full 22 months, give or take. During that time, the sight of helicopters and work crews drew lots of attention, both on the ground and in the newspapers. Progress reports were numerous, especially as construction drew to a close in the spring of 1963.[8]

As with any large-scale project such as the Tramway, the opening date was scheduled and re-scheduled numerous times. Originally, the opening was to be in April, 1963. As that date approached, a firmer date of May 15 was announced. However, a colder-than-normal late winter and early

Installing one of the many cables for the Palm Springs Aerial Tramway (Palm Springs Aerial Tramway photo).

spring resulted in colder-than-normal temperatures at the Mountain Station, plus low clouds that hindered visibility at the mountain.[9] Thus, in early May a new opening date of August 3 was announced.[10]

The August date turned out to be unacceptable for several reasons. Naturally, business concerns had issues with having such a big bash as the one planned during the hot summer months. The clincher came from Earl Coffman, who insisted that Governor "Pat" Brown be among the first to ride the new tram and inaugurate it. Governor Brown was not available during August, and so a new date was set of September 12. By then, the machinery would be tested, the system readied, the weather heading toward cooler months, and business interests could be prepared.[11]

In planning for the opening of the tram, it was decided that the ceremonies would be conducted over three days. On Thursday September 12, Governor Brown would be there to cut the ribbon and christen the first car up. He would be joined with a group of dignitaries known as the "Golden Fifty." These were politicians, celebrities, and other notables who would purchase special tickets at a price of $1,000 each to ride the first tram car up the mountain with the governor. The next day, more than 500 members of the media, mostly newspaper reporters and editors, would be given exclusive access to the tram, ride it for free, and be given a special gift. Obviously, their impressions were wanted so that they would in turn go back to their respective news outlets and write up their story of the tram, thus advertising the fact that it was finally opened. Finally, on Saturday, September 14, the Palm Springs Aerial Tramway would officially open to the public.

When September 12 arrived, the governor, his wife, and many dignitaries arrived for the official opening. The first car was loaded, the car was christened, and Governor Brown cut the ribbon to start the first passenger-carrying trip up the mountain. Over the next hour or so, more than 400 dignitaries, including mayors of several Southern California cities, Riverside County supervisors, Palm Springs City Council members, and some members of the press, all followed the "Golden

Postcard view of Governor Edmund G. "Pat" Brown cuting the ribbon on the inaugural run of the Palm Springs Aerial Tramway, September 12, 1963 (Author's collection).

(Above) Francis Crocker (left) and O. Earl Coffman stand at the plaque dedicating the opening of the Palm Springs Aerial Tramway, September 12, 1963 (Author's collection).

(Below) Dedication plaque today (Author's photo).

Fifty"[12] up the mountain where a large luncheon was provided, the guests were serenaded by a Swiss trio in Tyrolienne costumes, and a large Alpen horn was blown, giving the festivities an Alpine feel.[13]

The next day, the press corps (known as "newsboys") were given free reign of the tramway, and many were duly impressed. The Tramway received a lot of very worthwhile coverage.

Finally, on September 14, the Tramway was opened to the public. The charge for riding the tram for the public was $3.50 per adult on the weekdays, and $4.00 on the weekend, with children between the ages of 4 and 12 riding for $2.75 and $2.25 respectively. Children 4 years of age and younger rode for free.[14]

With the September 14 opening, the Palm Springs Aerial Tramway began its life as a major attraction in Riverside County and Southern California. Naturally, the opposition went their own ways, but in time, many grew to accept the new feature. Interestingly enough, even talking about the Tramway today elicits mixed emotions. Most, naturally, have lived their lives with the Tramway, and so know no other time when there was none. Many tourists take the Tramway for granted, but there is a certain subset of people who question whether approving and constructing the Tramway was a good idea. That idea grew very popular in the mid- and later-1960s during what can only be described as a very rocky and tenuous existence for the Tramway, but that is a subject for another work. Regardless of how one feels about the Tramway, it is here, and here it will stay.

Architect's rendering of the Mountain Station, 1963 (Palm Springs Aerial Tramway photo).

Architect's rendering of the Valley Station, 1963 (Palm Springs Aerial Tramway photo).

Aerial photo showing route of the Palm Springs Aerial Tramway and access road (Palm Springs Aerial Tramway photo).

Chapter 13 Endnotes

1. Davis, August 1973, p. 391.
2. *The Desert Sun*, September 28, 1960.
3. About $77 million in 2023 dollars.
4. Riverside *Press*, June 7, 1961.
5. Davis, August 1973, p. 419; Riverside *Press-Enterprise*, January 10, 1965.
6. Idyllwild *Town Crier*, June 9, 1961.
7. *The Desert Sun*, July 7, 1961.
8. The actual construction of the Palm Springs Aerial Tramway is a fascinating story by itself, but is beyond the scope of the present work. The reader who is interested in what it took to construct the tramway is highly encouraged to see James Landells' book entitled, *We Can Do It: The Construction of the Palm Springs Aerial Tramway*. Landells' father Don was one of the helicopter pilots who flew countless missions up and down the mountain delivering men and supplies to the various construction sites. He took hundreds of photographs during the two-year period, documenting most of the construction of the Tramway.
9. Most of the construction materials were still being lifted by helicopters which were very susceptible to visibility concerns given that multiple helicopters were operating in close proximity.
10. Idyllwild *Town Crier*, May 10, 1963.
11. It is during this time that quite unexpectedly, Francis Crocker resigned from the Mt. San Jacinto Winter Park Authority board. His explanation was that he wanted to take it easy, but speculation ran rampant that he resigned over the constant delay in opening the tram, culminating with Coffman's insistence that Governor Brown officiate at the grand opening, resulting in further delay. (Idyllwild *Town Crier*, June 21, 1963).
12. The "Golden Fifty" included Norman Dyhrenfurth, leader of the recent successful American expedition up Mt. Everest; Dinah Shore; Art Linkletter; Howard Duff; June Lockhart; members of the California State Parks and Beaches Commission; Senator and Mrs. Lee Backstrand, Assemblyman and Mrs. Gordon Cologne; Franklin S. Payne of the governor's Business Advisory Council; Los Angeles County Sheriff Peter Pitchess; Mrs. Dorothy Hicks of San Diego (winner of the popular "Queen For A Day" show); Fabian; and Beverly Garland. (*The Desert Sun*, September 12, 1963).
13. *The Desert Sun*, September 12, 1963.
14. *Ibid.*

Chapter 14

Final Thoughts

We finally went [on the tram], and enjoyed every minute of it, I hate to admit.

Nathan C. Clark, long-time official with the Sierra Club, 1977

Seems to me it would have been easier to have built a mountain for the tramway instead of building the tram up the mountain.

Unnamed construction worker as quoted in the Los Angeles Times, *September 8, 1963.*

In the previous pages, we've seen how the concept of the Palm Springs Aerial Tramway came into being, how it was approved, how it overcame countless obstacles, and how it handled the myriad of opposition to it to become one of Riverside County's most iconic attractions. While we of today take the existence of the Tramway for granted, the story of the opposition to the tramway is virtually unknown some 60 years after the Tramway's opening. However, it played a major role in shaping what the tramway was in the beginning, and what it is today.

So, we must ask ourselves – What of the opposition? Was it a wasted effort? Was it successful? Answering the latter question is kind of tricky and involves many aspects. Let's take a brief look at them.

Was the opposition successful? – No. Obviously, the point here is that despite all of the efforts to thwart the construction of the tramway, educating lawmakers and the public at large about the need for conservation, and the massive effort to show that the tramway would not be viable, the Tramway became a reality. In studying the story, it becomes obvious that the collective opposition to the tram was dealing with forces much bigger than it, and much better positioned and aligned than it. Crocker and Coffman were very well connected and had the backing, resources, and wherewithal to keep the project in the forefront and keep its perceived positive impacts in the minds of those whose opinion and position mattered. In short, the deck was stacked against the opposition from the beginning, and their late arrival in the planning process, together with their lack of organization and understanding of what they were up against hindered them greatly. In the end, despite their efforts, the tramway was constructed and remains to this day an integral part of the tourism industry in Riverside County.

Was the opposition successful? – Yes. The point here is to say that because of the opposition, the Tramway that was constructed looks nothing like the one initially proposed. The opposition's main arguments against constructing the tram centered mostly around protecting the high country of Mt. San Jacinto State Park and the Mt. San Jacinto Wilderness Area. Under the original proposal and mandate from the enabling legislation, much of Long Valley, Round Valley, and potentially the area around San Jacinto Peak would have become a major winter sports area, complete with ski lifts, sledding runs, restaurants, hotels/hostels, and other appurtenances. This would have had a major impact on the landscape. Certainly, it's been shown that the San Jacinto Mountains are not conducive to skiing, but constructing facilities for it, and then potentially not using them, would have been equally devastating. In the end, the opposition, by bringing awareness of conservation issues to the forefront, and working (either consciously or not) within the framework of the tramway's many delays, brought about an awareness among both local residents and others that what the San Jacinto Mountains offer is unique and should not be open to commercial exploitation. Sure, the tram has brought many thousands of people into the wilderness area who would not normally have gone there, but the impact could have been much, much worse had the project been developed as originally planned. Of course, the tramway DID get built, but in essence, the high country remained relatively unmolested, and for that, I believe we can say that the opposition was successful. As Nathan C. Clarke stated in 1977, "I think that, although we didn't win--we didn't keep the tramway out--we made a major impact, and I think the tramway that did go in is therefore, from my personal standpoint, perfectly acceptable."[1]

Regardless of what one may think of the pros and cons of the tramway and the opposition to it, it is my hope that the preceding pag-

Postcard view of the route of the Palm Springs Aerial Tramway, 1960s (Author's collection).

Publicity shot showing one of the original cars of the Palm Springs Aerial Tramway in use (Palm Springs Aerial Tramway photo).

es have shown the reader the one thing that struck me most in preparing this book, and that is the sheer tenacity and determination that both sides exhibited in the nearly 30 years that this project was in development. We have to recognize that many people, faced with the same set of obstacles and setbacks that the proponents tackled, would have given up long before they did. Seemingly one obstacle after another, from less-than-desirable bond markets to supply shortages to right-of-way issues, continued to plague the project, while the specter of a successful opposition campaign likewise swirled around them constantly. Through it all, though, they pursued the project, and were ultimately successful.

On the opposition end of the spectrum, their tenacity showed in their willingness and ability to continue to keep pressure on the State Legislature, local officials, and the public at large about the need for open-space recreation and how that very item was being threatened by so much development even in the 1950s. They were also able to bring to the forefront the argument against commercialization of State parks and other wilderness areas. They continued the fight, despite what we have seen were overwhelming odds. And when they experienced one defeat after another, they either regrouped and tried again, or a new group came in to pick up the pieces and continue the fight. In the end, the opposition got its message across, and the 25-year delay may have been their saving grace, because in that time, more conservation-minded people came into positions of power, which in turn meant that, when the original agreement expired and the Authority had to come back to the State with their hat in hand, leaders could exact a more conservation-minded agreement for the tramway, one that all but killed the notion of constructing a winter sports facility in the San Jacinto Mountains.

Advertising postcard for the Palm Springs Aerial Tramway, early 1960s (Author's collection).

Chapter 14 Endnotes

1. Clark, Nathan C., 1977, p. 101.

A Note About Trambi

Trambi was a cartoon squirrel mascot for the Palm Springs Aerial Tramway in the early 1960s. The Trambi cartoons found throughout this book were part of the original press packet handed out at the opening of the Tram (Palm Spring Aerial Tramway photo).

Appendices

APPENDIX A

REPORT OF PHIL KASPAR AND JIM MAYNARD REGARDING THEIR RECONNAISSANCE ALONG THE PROPOSED ROUTE

(Reproduced from The Desert Sun, *July 8, 1938)*

It is a dream now – but sometimes dreams come true; and it's very possible that Francis Crocker's vision of a tramway up the mountain to Round Valley will come true, provided his enthusiasm reaches an organization that can supply the do-re-me and the fa-so-la-ti.

Wednesday at approximately 2:30 a.m., Jim Maynard, the mountain climbing genius and I left Idyllwild for Mount San Jacinto, Round Valley, Long Valley and Hidden Lake to view the beauties a tramway would provide, and then to scamper down the mountainside to see the feasibility of erecting towers to carry the cable cars up the mountainside.

Looking down over the peak toward Palm Springs, one's soul is stirred with the grandeur at just the thought of riding through the air with the greatest of ease in a comfortable tram car, above the rough and rugged yet positively beautiful mountain country. To be so close and yet so far from such delightful country that now can only be reached by trail from Idyllwild is sad when we think about it, and how European countries, poor as they are, have over 70 such cable tramways, while poor, rich America so far has only one, and that recently installed in Franconia, New Hampshire, at a cost of $150,000.

Thrills, not only in summer, but also in winter, the valleys above hold for the winter guests and those interested in skiing, skating and tobogganing. Rising out of Palm Springs to the top of the peaks from warm sunshine to the cool and exhilarating breezes, the marvelous scenery of Round and Long Valleys is reached in 15 to 20 minutes or less to travel up the two-mile course. Sounds amazing, but it can be done, and I don't think Mr. Crocker will leave a stone unturned until his burned up ambition to ride a mountain tram may come true.

A word or two might be mentioned about the places of interest in this mountain rendezvous of hundreds of deer. The trails through this state park are in excellent condition and gradually sloped to make it easy to climb even the high mountain of San Jacinto, 10,865 feet in the sky.

The Sierra Hiking Club of Southern California built a stone cabin close to the peak, where travelers may use its cozy fireplace for warmth and a hot meal, and its double deck bunks to rest any bone that might be weary. At the peak there is a weather-protected steel container for notebooks, wherein the ambitious may record their deeds of ascension.

Coming down from the peak and strolling through the valley one sees besides the gigantic trees, fields of velvety grass, mountain rills, a campground once occupied by the C. C. C. that made the trails so pleasant to walk over, then the long valley with its beautiful, sloping country with shady and comforting places, quiet and peaceful.

Back a little ways is Hidden Lake formed by the snow waters of the mountains, a mirror for the trees to trim their foliage in, and off the lake a hundred feet a panorama of the entire valley is seen looking down directly into Tahquitz Canyon, an 8000-foot look, worth the price of the tramway ride. That will be an attractive dollar's worth of investment.

I had my trusty camera with me on this trip and when I say trusty, that's literally it. I slid with it 20 feet and it stayed with me, when my feet even left me. Coming down over the mountain close to the terminal of the proposed airway unlimited, the stalwart, rough, ready and lovable Jim Maynard proceeded to find trails down the treacherous mountainside, much to the comfort of the writer, who he kept bolstered up all along the route, singing in a deep bass voice, even semi-classical songs.

There are stepping stones of mountain all the way down from the peak and when you think you're near the end another boulder of magnificent proportions gets in your eyes and that means go over or around. The spirit was willing but the flesh was all in when the end was reached. The next time I traverse this hazardous country it will have to be on a tramway, because I don't feel like I can afford to risk another ten years of my life, not counting the ten pounds, pounded off making a 40-mile hike.

APPENDIX B

BREAKDOWN OF COSTS

(Reprinted from Modjeski & Masters, "Report on the Proposed Passenger Tramway up Mt. San Jacinto at Palm Springs, Cal," April 9, 1940)

PALM SPRINGS TRAMWAY
Estimate Cost of Project
400 Passengers per Hour Capacity

Tramway Materials Delivered	$	320,000.00
Foundations		160,000.00
Labor, Supervision and Erection Costs		150,000.00
Roadway Palm Springs to El. 2500		50,000.00
Lower Terminal Building		12,000.00
Upper Terminal Building		50,000.00
Water Supply Top		10,000.00
Sky ways, Paths and Recreation Facilities		20,000.00
Parking Areas for Autos		30,000.00
Design, Contract Plans, Contracts & Specifications		40,000.00
Supervision & Inspection during Construction		20,000.00
Inspection and Testing of Materials		10,000.00
Architects Fees		8,000.00
Real Estate and Property Rights		10,000.00
Legal Expenses		10,000.00
Bond Issue Expenses		15,000.00
Authority Expenses, Development		20,000.00
Administration Expenses		20,000.00
Publicity during Construction		5,000.00
Interest during Construction and Insurance		50,000.00
Contingencies during Construction		100,000.00
Total Project Cost		$1,310,000.00
Interest Reserve and Working Capital		50,000.00
Total Financing Required		$1,360,000.00
Estimated Gross Revenues		$300,000.00
Estimated Operating Cost		130,000.00
Net for Service of Bonds		$170,000.00

APPENDIX C

HARRY JAMES' LETTER TO PRESIDENT FRANKLIN DELANO ROOSEVELT REQUESTING NATIONAL MONUMENT STATUS FOR MT. SAN JACINTO AND MT. SAN GORGONIO

(Harry C. James papers (MS 111). Special Collections & University Archives, University of California, Riverside)

June 7, 1943

The Honorable Franklin Delano Roosevelt
President of The United States,
The White House,
Washington, D. C.

My dear Mr. President:

As President of The Trailfinders, an outdoor organization for boys, I would like to urge the setting aside of Mt. San Jacinto and Mt. San Gorgonio as national Monuments.

These two mountains and the surrounding territory are just about the only true wilderness areas left in the mountains of southern California, and only by such action can they be preserved for posterity in their pristine beauty. Both areas have many unique features which, in our estimation, make them worthy for consecration as National Monuments.

First: They are unique in exhibiting a climatic cross-section of North America from Alaska to Canada.

Second: Mt. San Jacinto and Mt. San Gorgonio provide biologists with a unique field for the study of animal and plant distribution through the various life zones from the Lower Sonoran of the Colorado Desert to the Arctic-Alpine Zone of the mountain summits.

Third: The preservation of such areas as National Monuments will preserve for all time two rather spectacular wilderness areas against the nosy constant threat of development. Hardly a year passes without some attempt being made to break into the present Forest Service restrictions as Primitive Areas.

Fourth: With the status of National Monuments the public would have access to them for such recreation as would not jeopardize the true wilderness character of the areas.

Fifth: San Jacinto and San Gorgonio, 10,805 feet and 11,485 feet respectively in altitude, have stood like sentinels over the two great passes into southern California. They have witnessed every exploring expedition from De Anza and Jedediah Smith to the early Mormon scouts. They have historical significance.

Sixth: In the lower altitudes surrounding both mountains are innumerable children's camps. The wilderness areas afford priceless opportunities for nature study, mountain climbing, horseback trips, and all the other recreations. These values should be preserved for children for all time.

We, therefore, urge the transference of their present status as Primitive Areas to that of National Monuments.

Sincerely yours,
Harry C. James

APPENDIX D

WILDERNESS RECREATION FOR A METROPOLITAN AREA
by Joe R. Momyer

(Reprinted from the Sierra Club Bulletin, Vol. 34, No. 8; September, 1949, pp. 4–6)

FEW PEOPLE REALIZE that within four hours of downtown Los Angeles by car and on foot one can be in a beautiful and unspoiled mountain wilderness into which one may hike or ride horseback and enjoy alpine scenery and environment. This very proximity to a major metropolitan area gives real value to the Mount San Jacinto State Park and Wild Area.

In an area rivaled only by Florida for literally hundreds of fine beaches with added mountain, desert, and valley resorts and clubs, the San Jacinto region has an irreplaceable value. For Southern California can provide very little of the type of wilderness experience San Jacinto offers to mountain lovers. The mountains are ideally situated, in the center of the six southern counties, to provide this rare form of recreation for those who wish it among the large and rapidly growing population.

All the official Wild Areas in Southern California put together cover less area than Yosemite National Park. The combined San Jacinto State Park and Forest Service Wild Area account for about one fourth of all the acreage reserved in these wild areas, yet it equals only a half of one per cent of the land area in the six southern counties. The State Park alone, which includes the most beautiful high portion of the San Jacinto Mountains, accounts for fully one half of the fine alpine country available in the south, yet it represents only .00048 per cent of the land area of the six southern counties.

"But what does wilderness recreation mean?" one is asked. That is a fair question and a hard one to answer. It means the anticipation and fun of planning a trip, checking sleeping bags and knapsacks, studying maps, choosing lightweight foods to provide nourishment without excess weight, planning the itinerary and learning where good sleeping spots, water, and firewood will be–above all, the gathering together of a group of friends, kindred spirits, who sense that the degree of appreciation of a grand mountain scene is based largely on the extent to which it is earned, that one must participate in an experience, not merely be a passive spectator.

"Wilderness experience on San Jacinto," in terms of an individual hiker, means sticking one's nose out of a warm sleeping bag into the cool mountain morning, the delicious aroma of bacon frying over a wood fire. It means shouldering a not-too heavy pack and swinging light-heartedly up the forest trail through alders, oaks, and cottonwood; then gradually into incense cedar, juniper, big-cone spruce, white fir, and the grand straight pines—ponderosa, Jeffrey, sugar and Coulter. It means gradually climbing the switchbacks of the Devil's Slide trail, seeing the gentle, forested valley lying cupped below, with an occasional wisp of smoke to mark the beginning of the day in some cabin beneath the trees, wondering at the great granite upthrust of Tahquitz Rock and rugged Tahquitz Peak.

Crossing the saddle at the top of the stiff climb brings one to another, more remote, more peaceful world. There are no signs of man or his works here except the well-worn foot trail. An occasional disturbed chipmunk or curious gray squirrel races up a tree, scolding at the intrusion; and a flash of movement betrays a startled lizard. By now the sun is warm and one sinks gratefully onto a grassy bank beside a stream of mountain water that crosses the trail at a green cienaga, perhaps occasionally to see a graceful deer and her fawn step into the open on the far side of the meadow.

Then pack on the shoulders again—a pack, lightened somewhat now as a result of trailside snacks, and on toward the summit of the great mountain. The faint squeaking of the leather straps on the knapsack and the occasional shrilling of a cricket are in good harmony in the pine-scented air, while the greenness of the trees and shrubs is brightened by azaleas.

Eventually, after pleasant sun-drenched miles of trail, broken by occasional other peaceful rests on shady, pine-needle covered hillsides, one finally is on the summit, and knows the climber's exhilaration, that must be experienced to be understood. One gazes on the vastness of mountain ranges and the sweep of the desert below. He feels his perspective improve as he stands there.

The trip down may be made the same day; or one may sleep out under the pines. On the down trail one crosses lovely meadows, stops to look at Hidden Lake (dry this year), and hikes for long stretches, in Tahquitz Valley, through ferns reaching shoulder-high. Back at the foot of the trail, the car cushions feel feather-soft, and the whole body is deliciously tired with a wholesome fatigue. An invigorating bath and hot food perform miracles, however, and soon thoughts are racing to plans for another trip and to memories of peaceful sunlit meadows remote from daily tensions and strains. As Thoreau said over 90 years ago: "Our life would stagnate if it were not for the unexplored forests and meadows which surround it. We need the tonic of the wilderness. We can never have enough of nature. We must be refreshed by the sight of the inexhaustible vigor ... of the wilderness with its living and decaying trees."

In considering the recreational values of such an area, the experiences of the individual hiker must be multiplied by the thousands of people who use the area in its present form each year. There are fifty organized groups (Boy and Girl Scouts, YMCA and YWCA groups, and so on) using campsites in the Idyllwild area. Annually, approximately 16,000 people now use the area for an average of a day and a half each—approximately 24,000 man days per year. Surely this is a valid utilization of great importance to Southern California. True, it is not a mass utilization. Nevertheless, a distinctive and rare bit of mountain wilderness should be entitled to as much consideration and protection as a unique bit of desert, a richly carved stretch of beach, a museum, or a great library. Each serves a portion of the public; each fills a need, and neither should squeeze out the other.

We need to think in terms of permanent recreational values for the people who *live* in Southern California rather than in terms of added superficial attractions to bring a greater flood of transient tourists through the state. If we make Southern California a desirable place in which to live, enough tourists will still visit us and many of them will stay to become permanent residents.

SHOULD WE CHERISH AND MAINTAIN THE SAN JACINTO WILD AREA?

by Guy L. Fleming

(Reprinted from the Sierra Club Bulletin, Vol. 34, No. 9; October, 1949, pp. 4 – 10)

IF THE ANSWER to the title of this article is *Yes!* and we do believe it is the wish of the People of California to cherish and protect its Wild Areas, those few remaining remnants of its unique native landscape—our desire must be formulated and forcefully expressed now, before actual construction of the San Jacinto Tramway is started.

Public opinion can prevent the construction of the proposed tramway into the San Jacinto Wild Area. It is reported that the project awaits clearance by court action to establish the validity of its revenue bonds. Public opposition to the project can affect the bond issue.

Let us recall the effective and successful public opposition against opening up the San Gorgonio Wild Area to commercial exploitation.

The campaign must be aggressive. There are abundant facts on which to base it.

THE ACT of 1945, creating the Mount San Jacinto Winter Park Authority and "prescribing the powers and duties thereof," carries the statement in the preamble: "The people of the State of California do enact as follows: . . . There is in the State Park System Mount San Jacinto State Park, which is owned by the State and which is ideally situated for winter sports, including skiing . . . which affords unlimited opportunities for healthful recreation in a snow area immediately adjacent to the desert recreational area of Palm Springs. These conditions are special and peculiar to this park and do not exist in any other park in the State Park System." It is true that in its nearness to the resort of Palm Springs "these conditions are special and peculiar to this park."

The Act cites that Mount San Jacinto State Park is so inaccessible (to Palm 'Springs) that "in order to raise funds for its improvement . . . it is essential that a special authority" (other than the State Division of Beaches and Parks) "must be created" and "thereby make available to the people of California the winter and other recreational facilities of Mount San Jacinto State Park."

Mount San Jacinto was acquired and set aside as a wilderness park, and so dedicated June 19, 1937, for the express purpose of protecting and holding, in perpetuity, an outstanding example of unique mountain wilderness. It was realized when this area was purchased that it contained wilderness values that are intangible and extremely fragile. The very fact that it could not withstand heavy public concentrated resort-type use inspired the policy that it would be dedicated as "a wilderness reservation."

THE San Jacinto Mountains are the southernmost area of true alpine flora in the Southwest States. This mountain of all mountains in the United States represents practically all of the life zones of the American continent.

The natural aspects of this area and their value to the scientist and to the average citizen were summed up many years ago by the late Dr. Harvey Monroe Hall in his publication of "A Botanical Survey of San Jacinto Mountain," issued by the University of California Press in 1902. This survey covered a five-year period (1896-1901) and gives a detailed account of the meadows, forests, and natural features of fifty years ago. At that time Dr. Hall described the delicate ecological balance of this region. Today it is about as unspoiled as it was in 1900.

The flora of Mount San Jacinto represents a meeting place of the alpine plants which have migrated southward via the Sierra Nevada and the Sierra Madre ranges and the northward and westward movement of desert forms from Mexico, New Mexico, and Arizona.

Five life zones completely encircle San Jacinto. And on the northeastern slopes, wholly within the State Park, we have six life zones very much crowded together, from the Sonoran in Chino Canyon to the alpine on the top of San Jacinto (10,805 feet). The four upper zones of the mountain almost overlap one another. Dr. Hall stated: "There is probably no place in North America where the alpine and the Sonoran floras are in such proximity as they are on San Jacinto Mountain."

All conservators who advocate the protection of unique and special types of native landscape know the delicate balance that exists between plant associations in these exceptional areas.

The impact of the intensive "development" in the proposed program of the Mount San Jacinto Winter Park Authority will cause greater and longer lasting damage to this area than would a major fire or some natural cataclysm.

Once the mountain is opened up to uncontrolled and intensive public use, by the invasion of the tramway into the heart of its unique wilderness, the special values that make this area unusual will be gone forever.

The promoters of the tramway project have stated: "The preservation of the spirit of the wilderness is of paramount importance to the tramway committee and its members. It seeks to destroy none of the primitive features of the Park, but is interested solely in making the Park accessible to the public by use of the tramway as a means of transportation into the area.

It is not understandable how it will be possible to construct over two miles of high-line tram-cableway into the very heart of the wilderness area, with attendant towers, terminals, and other man made appurtenances, without absolutely destroying "the spirit of the wilderness." In planning to cater to the hundreds of people the tramway promoters expect to bring into the park daily, winter and summer, they contemplate building "ski-houses, ski hostels (hotels), upskis, ski lifts, power lines, roads," and so on.

The development of necessary water supplies for the heavy concentration of public use will rob the springs, stream courses, and meadows of their water, and the associated vegetation of their life source. These things are permitted in the contract of the Mount San Jacinto Winter Park Authority. This proposed development can only result in the destruction "of the primitive features of the park."

IT is too commonly believed that the highest utilization of the land for the greatest number of people is valid justification and warrants the modification of selected areas for intensive recreational purposes. The interrelationships are so delicate and the associations so fragile in many of these "select" areas that the removal of one factor may frequently disrupt the entire biological equilibrium. Far too often have we seen overenthusiastic planners plunge into the problem of developing recreation areas hoping to bring the beauties of some unique area within easy reach of the public, only to find that in the end they have, by doing so, robbed it of the very charm that they sought to reveal.

The record is clear that it was the intention of those who collaborated in the creation of Mount San Jacinto State Park that it was to be maintained "as a wilderness reservation for the public." The following chronological outline of events gives proof that the founders of this Wilderness State Park obtained the lands which constitute this Park solely upon the condition that the entire State owned area would be dedicated as part of the San Jacinto Wild Area.

Early in 1919 Mr. A. C. Lovekin, a former resident of the City of Riverside, and then an active member of the Riverside Chapter of the Sierra Club, advocated setting aside the higher altitudes of the San Jacinto range and Riverside Palm Canyon as a World War Monument, a great wilderness memorial park to honor those who gave their lives in World War I. In June, 1919, Mr. Lovekin went to Washington, D.C., at the request of the Riverside Board of Supervisors, and there succeeded in having legislation passed which set aside approximately sixteen hundred acres in Palm Canyon as a National Monument. However, the Act was conditional and provided "that the Palm Canyon, which embraces Indian lands, shall become a National Monument in fact when the Indians have agreed to sell their lands at an appraisal price decided upon by the Indian agent."

Mr. Lovekin's vision of a great wilderness memorial park met with general public approval, but it was not until 1927, after the State Legislature passed the Statutes of 1927, creating a State Park System, that the plan for a Mount San Jacinto wilderness park became an active program, with the support of all of Southern California.

In the fall of 1927, Governor C. C. Young appointed the following persons to serve on the first State Park Commission: Mr. William E. Colby, Secretary of the Sierra Club, Chairman; Dr. Ray Lyman Wilbur, President of Stanford University; Ex-Senator W. F. Chandler, of Fresno; Mr. Henry W. O'Melveny, of Los Angeles; and Major Frederick R. Burnham, of Los Angeles. An outstanding group of true conservators and sincere advocates of retaining as the heritage of the people of California unusual and superior examples of this Commonwealth's unique native landscape.

This Commission held its first meeting in Sacramento on December 13th, 1927. It is believed that at this meeting the Park Commission endorsed the selection of Frederick Law Olmsted, internationally known, and now America's Dean of Landscape Engineering, as Director of the California State Park Survey, and set up the policies for carrying on the State-wide park survey.

At this time Mr. Newton B. Drury, Secretary of the Save-the-Redwoods League, was drafted as Investigating and Acquisition Officer to collaborate in the State Park program. Mr. Drury served in this capacity until 1940, when he became Director of the National Park Service.

In 1927 the late Albert E. Bottel, then Riverside County Agricultural Commissioner and Chairman of the Riverside County Board of Forestry, carried on an active campaign to interest the people of Southern California in supporting a program to have Mount San Jacinto included in the list of possible State Parks.

On January 26th, 1928, the Riverside County Board of Forestry called a public meeting at the Riverside Court House. Mr. Bottel, in concluding his address proposing that the Mount San Jacinto area be acquired as a unit of the State Park System, stated: "If, after a full discussion of the Matter today it is decided by this delegation that the proposed plan is feasible and that we should make every effort to secure a State Park, it would appear to me to be advisable to appoint a committee from this meeting to head the entire proposition . . After discussion by the citizens present a resolution was presented which concluded as follows:

> Be it herewith resolved, that this Committee be instructed to present a plan to the State Park Commission and request their cooperation in working out a program for financing this project should the State Park bond issue be carried by the people in the November election.

A committee of ten persons from Riverside County, under the leadership of Mr. A. C. Lovekin and Dr. E. P. Clarke, of the Riverside Daily Press, attended the State Park Commission meeting in Los Angeles, February 8, 1928, and submitted their proposal that an area of the San Jacinto Mountains be included in the State Park System.

Further meetings were held in Riverside and it was decided to found and incorporate the San Jacinto State Park Association. The incorporation was completed September 22, 1928, and the following officers were elected: A. C. Lovekin, President; H. W. Postlethwaite, 1st Vice-President; W. L. Pollar, 2d Vice-President; R. C. Harbison, 3d Vice-President; A. E. Bottel, Secretary; Jonas Killian, Treasurer. Twenty-four directors were selected representing the Southern California counties. Of this directorate the following formed the Executive Committee: Dr. E. P. Clarke; A. H. Winder; J. E. McGregor; J. R. Gabbert, and A. C. Lovekin.

Among the well-known persons who served as directors were: the late Harry Chandler, owner and publisher of the Los Angeles Times; Dr. George P. Clements, Agricultural Dept., Los Angeles Chamber of Commerce; the late Frank Miller, owner of the famous Riverside Mission Inn; Howard H. Hays, Riverside publisher; and Mrs. Nellie Coffman, owner of the Desert Inn, Palm Springs.

At the general election of November, 1928, the people of California overwhelmingly ratified the State Park Bond Act which provided for the issuance of $6,000,000 in state bonds to be used for the purchase of park lands, with the definite stipulation that state funds must be matched, dollar for dollar, by funds or lands from sources other than the state.

Prominent park and forest engineers worked with the San Jacinto State Park Association in furthering the general plan of acquisition of lands for the proposed park. Matching funds for the project were pledged by the Riverside Board of Supervisors and private citizens. At the time the odd-numbered sections of land in the San Jacinto Mountains were Southern Pacific lands or in other private ownership, while the even-numbered sections were federally owned lands of the Forest Service.

AT THE MEETING of the State Park Commission, March 25, 1929, Mr. Frederick L. Olmsted presented his Statement in Regard to the Region Culminating in the San Jacinto Mountains, which was adopted as the general guide in the acquisition of the lands for Mount San Jacinto State Park and the creation of the present San Jacinto Wild Area. The preamble of this Statement and the recommended plan of acquisition of lands for the State Park is here reported:

> Preamble: As a basis for discussion there is here presented a tentative outline of a broad and comprehensive public policy, relating not merely to a proposed State Park in the San Jacinto Mountains, but to the future utilization of the natural resources of the entire mountainous region of which the San Jacinto Range is the culmination, a region of which the total area that can be reasonably made a state park is a relatively small fraction.
>
> Acquisition Procedure: What is contemplated as a practical proposition in regard to the San Jacinto range, as the culminating mountain feature of the region, is substantially as follows:
>
> 1. That the State Park Commission shall secure control by purchase, or condemnation where necessary, and by gift in whole or in part where possible, of all private lands, that is to say all lands not held by the United States Government as part of the National Forest, within an area in the San Jacinto Mountains as large as the funds which shall become available will permit, embracing as of first importance the higher and wilder parts of the mountains in the area known as the Tahquitz Game Preserve, but extending out from that nucleus to include those lands that are well adapted for the free public enjoyment of the mountains and which are not so encroached upon by existing resort developments or so peculiarly well adapted to private use as to make the price of acquirement excessive. The State's expenditures out of the bond issue funds will be limited to an amount not in excess of other contributions from other sources in money and in value of lands tendered in gift, the valuations at which land is taken over, either by gift or by purchase, being limited to the amount of fair and careful appraisals made by or for the Commission.
>
> 2. That the necessarily interrupted holding thus acquired by the State from private owners shall be consolidated by a process of exchange with the Forest Service, with a view (a) to creating one or more large continuous bodies of State Park land suitable in location and boundary for satisfactory use and administration . . . and (b) creating in contact with the State Park land a similarly Consolidated body of continuous National Forest land, definitely withdrawn as a "Wilderness Area," in which any

lumbering operations or building operations or road construction shall be permanently prohibited and which shall be administered for public recreation of kinds suitable for a wilderness by the Forest Service, with close cooperation between the State Park Service and the National Forest Service in trail building, protection and policing on both areas considered as one functional unit, to the extent permitted by funds annually available to each.

The National Forest Service is in thorough agreement with the general program above outlined. The State Park Commission is prepared to hold available for application to such a program an adequate portion of the bond issue funds long enough to give reasonable opportunity for raising the contributory funds. The next step is to begin negotiations for the land acquirement by gift and by purchase.

The State of California Makes a Promise

The program outlined by Mr. Olmsted was carried forward. On October 23, 1950, Mr. William E. Colby, Chairman of the State Park Commission, addressed a letter to the Board of Supervisors of Riverside County reporting upon the progress of the acquisition of the area desired for a State Park, and in the third paragraph stated:

> The acquisition of these lands by the State will result from a three-cornered transaction involving the Southern Pacific Land Company, the United States Forest Service and the State Park Commission, whereby the Southern Pacific Land Company, through trading land with the U. S. Forest Service will obtain in a consolidated block the lands which they will then sell to the State of California. This procedure was necessary because of the legal restrictions which made it impossible for the U. S. Forest Service to purchase lands or for the State Park Commission to secure lands by exchange. As a result of the exchange and purchase agreed upon, not only will the Mount San Jacinto State Park be established but all of the Railroad holdings within this area of some 33,000 acres will have been acquired either by the State or by the U. S. Forest Service and *this entire area centering about San Jacinto Peak and Tahquitz Peak will he held as a wilderness reservation for the benefit of the public.* [Italics ours.]

In closing his letter to the Riverside Board of Supervisors Mr. Colby wrote:

> On behalf of the State Park Commission, permit me to express our deep appreciation of the generous way in which Riverside County has rallied to the support of the Mount San Jacinto Project. We are happy that it is so near completion, and believe that it will be an outstanding asset to your County and to the State.

The valuation of the 12,695 acres within Mount San Jacinto State Park, acquired from the Southern Pacific Land Company and the U. S. Forest Service, was $84,218.75. One half of this sum was contributed by Riverside County and friends of the park project.

Sometime prior to Mr. Colby's letter to the Riverside Board of Supervisors, the U. S. Regional Forester, in San Francisco, in a communication to the Chief Forester, in Washington, D.C., dated Oct. 1, 1930, reported:

> If this transaction goes through it is the plan of the State Park Commission to maintain their land as a part of the combined San Jacinto Mountain State Park-Forest Service Primitive Area of about 32,000 acres.

In 1937, during the C.C.C. program, the State Park Commission and the Forest Service were urged to construct roads into the high country.

On June 12, 1937, Mr. Newton B. Drury, State Park Acquisition Officer, submitted a memorandum to Mr. Joseph R. Knowland, Chairman of the State Park Commission at that time on the subject, "Suggested Automobile Road to Summit of Mt. San Jacinto." Mr. Drury advised Mr. Knowland:

> When Mt. San Jacinto State Park was established in 1933, while there was no formal action by the State Park Commissoin, a tacit understanding was reached with the U. S. Forest Service and the proponents of the project that the entire park area of approximately 12,700 acres would be administrated as a "primitive region," to be penetrated only by foot and horse trails. There has been no plan for an automobile road to the summit.

In a communication from the office of the Regional Forester, San Francisco, dated June 15, 1937, Mr. Drury received assurance from that agency that it had no intention of constructing roads into the San Jacinto Wild Area. The following statement from that communication is very specific:

The policy of the Forest Service is to preserve the San Jacinto primitive area as a road-less one, and it has always been our understanding that the San Jacinto State Park would be kept in a similar status. When the land exchange with the Southern Pacific Land Company was submitted as a step in the consolidation of the State Park, it was approved by our Washington office and the Secretary with the understanding that the entire area, both Federal and State, would remain roadless.

Mr. Knowland, the chairman of the Park Commission, reaffirmed the policy of preserving the wilderness character of Mount San Jacinto State Park in a public address, which was reported by the *Riverside Daily Press*, June 19, 1937:

"State policies" was the subject of Knowland's address. He declared that "the retention of the park as a wilderness would always be the policy of the State Park Commission."

The last published record is the minutes of the State Park Commission of June 27, 1937, stating that the Commission, "unanimously adopted the policy of the National Forest Service in the preservation of the San Jacinto Primitive Area."

The references to the creation of Mount San Jacinto State Park set forth in this chronological outline give us assurance that the Park was made possible upon the condition that it would be a part of the dedicated San Jacinto Wild Area, and that it would be held as such in perpetuity, as "trail country"—a primitive wilderness without artificial development. It is upon this premise that the people of California must make their case against the commercial agencies that seek to exploit natural wilderness resources for financial gain.

IF IT is the will and desire of the People of California to retain Mount San Jacinto State Park as a wilderness area, and be assured that its primitive aspects will be held in perpetuity they must be aggressive in pressing their case upon the grounds that the State Legislature in creating the Mount San Jacinto Winter Park Authority violated a definite and publicly expressed agreement made in good faith between the State Park Commission, representing the people of California, and the United States Forest Service, representing the people of this nation, that Mount San Jacinto be a definite part of the federally dedicated San Jacinto Wild Area and subject to the policies accepted for the protection and maintenance of established wilderness areas.

THE MOUNT SAN JACINTO TRAMWAY SCHEME
by Guy L. Fleming

(Reprinted from the National Parks Magazine, Vol. 23, No. 97, pp. 21 – 25: April-June, 1949).

THE towering San Jacinto Mountains constitute one of the outstanding remnants of true wilderness in southern California. This region, dedicated in 1930 as a federal-state primitive area through a joint agreement between the U. S. Forest Service and the California State Park Commission, was set aside as a wilderness reserve, free from the pressures of "too much civilization," accessible only by foot and horse trails for the people of California and the nation.

Today, resort hotel owners and commercial interests of Palm Springs and nearby communities look up at the cool, forested slopes of Mount San Jacinto, whose summit is over 10,000 feet above Palm Springs, and visualize making it publicly accessible, but in a way that would wipe out its wilderness charm. Because trails on the precipitous east slopes are impractical, they propose to construct an aerial tramway up into the wilderness area.

The Forest Service-Park Commission agreement originated in 1928, when a group of Riverside County citizens sponsored establishment of a state park in the San Jacinto Mountains. Through a land transaction between the Southern Pacific Land Company, owner of railroad lands in the San Jacinto Mountains, the U. S. Forest Service and the California State Park Commission, a three-cornered land exchange was evolved. By it the State of California acquired over 12,000 acres of the higher part of the San Jacinto Mountains, including San Jacinto Peak, elevation 10,805 feet, Marion and Jean peaks. over 10,000 feet, forested slopes, high mountain meadows, in fact, the very heart of the wilderness area. The Forest Service in turn obtained two consolidated blocks of land totaling over 23,000 acres, one unit lying to the north of Mount San Jacinto State Park, embracing the precipitous north slopes of San Jacinto Mountain, including rugged, picturesque Snow Canyon and its forks, and equally rugged and picturesque Chino Canyon. The second unit of consolidated Forest Service lands lie south of the state park and include Tahquitz Peak, Tahquitz Valley, broad benches, with unspoiled stands of ponderosa pine, and the scenic canyon of Willow Creek.

Thus was established the San Jacinto Wild Area—a primitive public reserve of over 36,000 acres.

There are several existing references to the understanding between the Forest Service and the State Commission that Mount San Jacinto State Park is a unit of the federal-state San Jacinto wild area:

(1)A communication from the regional forester, in San Francisco, to the chief forester, in Washington, D. C., dated October 1, 1930, containing the following sentence:

> "If this transaction goes through it is the plan of the State Park Commission to maintain their land as a part of the combined San Jacinto Mountain State Park-Forest Service Primitive Area of about 32,000 acres."

(2) A letter from Mr. William E. Colby, chairman of the first California State Park Commission to the Riverside County Board of Supervisors, dated October 23, 1930, containing the following:

> "As a result of the exchange and purchase agreed upon, not only will the Mount San Jacinto State Park be established, but all the railroad holdings within this area of some 33,000 acres will have been acquired either by the state or the Forest Service, and this entire area centering about San Jacinto Peak and Tahquitz will be held as a wilderness reserve for the benefit of the public."

(3) A public address by Mr. J. R. Knowland, chairman of the State Park Commission under the Merriam administration, and reported by the Riverside Daily Press of June 19, 1937:

> "State policies was the subject of Knowland's address. He declared that the retention of the park as a wilderness area would always be the policy of the State Park Commission."

(4) The last published record is the minutes of the State Park Commission meeting of June 27, 1937, saying that the Commission, "unanimously adopted the policy of the National Park Service in the preservation of the San Jacinto Primitive Area."

It is apparent from the above references that the creation of Mount San Jacinto State Park was accomplished with the cooperation of the U. S. Forest Service on the condition that the park would be a part of a dedicated wilderness reserve.

During the summers of 1934, -35. -36 and -37, the National Park Service, with the cooperation of the State Division of Parks, maintained CCC units in Mount San Jacinto State Park. The federal work project developed twenty miles of trail in the park, built a stone refuge house on San Jacinto Peak, provided camping facilities in Round Valley, and constructed a park ranger's cottage and campground and picnic ground facilities for the park administration site at Idyllwild. Federal expenditures for the periods cited totaled approximately $250.000.

The federal-state wilderness area now provides nearly forty miles of well-developed trails. For years, thousands of people have passed over these trails and have experienced the pleasure of being explorers of the primitive high country.

In 1945, a Palm Springs organization, known as the "Mount San Jacinto Tramway Committee," with the backing of the State Chamber of Commerce and the California All Year Club, sponsored an Assembly Bill, which, with the support of a very strong lobby, headed by a prominent Los Angeles attorney, passed both houses of the state legislature and was signed by Governor Warren. The many organizations and individuals opposing the tramway plan were not articulate enough to offset the power politics used by the promoters of the project. In fact, the advocates for the retention of the wilderness aspects of Mount San Jacinto State Park may have relied too strongly upon the fact that the State Park Commission, composed entirely of native Californians, would uphold the agreement made by their predecessors in office that the park "he held as a wilderness reserve for the benefit of the public." Furthermore, they intended to persuade Governor Warren, also a native Californian, to veto the bill.

The 1945 bill was an enabling act permitting creation of the Mount San Jacinto Winter Park Authority - "a public agency and a public corporation of the State of California." The authority is empowered to issue revenue bonds, without limit of issue and tax exempt, "to carry out the objects and purposes of the act."

The act provides that the authority may construct and complete roads, tramways, aerial cableways, up-skis, ski-lifts, ski huts, ski hostels, restaurants, and other "works" useful for the "development of winter sports and any other recreational facilities within the territorial limits of the authority" but, "provided further, that any of the powers granted herein shall be exercised within the territorial limits of Mount San Jacinto Stale Park only by the express consent and under contract with the State Park Commission."

The act gave the authority territorial jurisdiction over almost all of the federal and state lands within the San Jacinto wild area, including 22,120 acres of Forest Service land and 7680 acres of Mount San Jacinto State Park, the latter embracing the choicest part of the wilderness country, including San Jacinto Peak, Marion Peak, Round Valley and Hidden Lake.

Representatives of the Mount San Jacinto Winter Park Authority appeared before the Park Commission at a meeting held in Los Angeles, December 17, 1948, and formally requested approval of a contract with the State Park Commission to proceed with the construction of that part of the proposed tramway which must pass over state park lands, and for the construction of the upper tramway terminal facilities at Long Valley, in the very heart of the wilderness section of the park. Delegations representing the Sierra Club, the Federation of Western Outdoor clubs, and other conservation organizations of Southern California, also the National Parks Association, represented by a Los Angeles member, Mr. Martin Litton, were present at the December meeting. They requested the Park Commission to deny the contract, inasmuch as a concession granting the Winter Park Authority a contract to construct a cable tramway, with its attendant towers and other appurtenances, onto and over state park lands would be a violation of a policy established by former park commissions, which dedicated the entire Mount Sari Jacinto area, both federal and state lands, as a wilderness free from artificial means of access.

The conservation delegation was informed by the State Park Commission that the legislative act of 1945, creating the Mount San Jacinto Winter Park Authority, was a mandate from the state legislature requiring the Park Commission to enter into a contract with the authority to construct the tramway. The Commission further stated, however, that the terms of the legislative act gave the Commission "powers to protect the primitive area against damage by tramway construction and operation."

How the State Park Commission can save "the primitive area from damage" under the proposed scheme is difficult to understand.

The project would construct eight or more tremendous cable towers. One, for example, would have a base area of 117 by seventy feet, straddling the Chino Canyon ridge at the 5600-foot level, and rising 275 feet above the ridge. Three terminal structures would be established at the 2650-foot, 5600-foot and 8500-foot levels. At the upper and lower terminals, the cables would run into deep wells, where machinery would keep them at proper tension to offset contraction and expansion. The tramway would rise more than 5800 feet in a horizontal distance of 10,700 feet. The complete project would include a spacious station terminal in Long Valley, with waiting rooms, restaurant and over-night rooms, plus other facilities to cater to "the expected throngs who will visit this new scenic wonderland." It is obvious that once the wilderness is penetrated by this transportation facility, pressure will be brought upon the Park Commission for construction of roads in the upper altitudes, and that the landscape will be spoiled by clearing for ski areas, ski-lifts, cabins and large public campgrounds. In short, the people of California and the nation will lose another primitive area.

Before tramway construction can be started, the Winter Park Authority must make application to the U. S. Forest Service for a permit to cross over part of the federally owned lands of the San Jacinto Wild Area. Under the law creating primitive and wild areas, the Chief of the U. S. Forest Service must call a public hearing before status or boundaries of such a reservation can be altered. It was this law that afforded the public the opportunity to prevent commercial invasion and modification of the San Gorgonio Primitive Area two years ago. (See NATIONAL PARKS MAGAZINE, numbers 89 and 90).

Assembly Bill 1337 has been introduced in the 1949 session of the state legislature for the purpose of repealing the 1945 act creating the Mount San Jacinto Winter Park authority. All California advocates of the retention of our wilderness areas should write to their state legislative representatives at Sacramento and urge them to support the repeal bill.

The Mount San Jacinto Wild Area can be saved! It is our privilege and our duty to keep it inviolate for generations to come.

APPENDIX E

EDITORIALS

(Reprinted from the Riverside Enterprise, April 20, 1950)

Tramway Called Threat to Democracy

Editor Press and Enterprise: Sometimes I wonder how long democracy can endure in this country—and my worry is not based on the activities of the Communists. Their weird machinations will no more convert us than did the insane burblings of the Nazis. What is rather to be expected is that our people will gradually cease to believe in democracy, will come to think that money interests and pressure groups are too powerful to resist and that the common man is helpless before them. When that time comes, the Communists can take over without firing a hydrogen bomb.

These gloomy reflections come from reading your editorial last week on the Palm Springs Tramway. You say "we think that the benefit from the enjoyment of the tramway will outweigh the detriment from the invasion of the mountain area."

Doesn't it make any difference to you that the park to be invaded was created with lands and money donated on the promise that the park would be preserved as a primitive area? Chairman Knowland put himself on record, according to the Riverside Press of June 19, 1937, by saying that the retention of the park as a wilderness would always be the policy of the State Park Commission.

If this magnificent mountain, set aside as a primitive area and promised protection by the State of California, can be invaded and taken over by a commercial enterprise, confidence in representative government will be weakened again. Where does it leave the common man, whose heritage of wild nature is destroyed to make money for Palm Springs promoters?

Greedy and prehensile men cannot be expected to value properly the gifts of nature, to understand the loss to coming generations robbed of the virgin forests and meadows which up to now have been the background of American life. But we had a right to expect something better from a paper with the tradition of public service established by Dr. E. P. Clarke. One cannot imagine his excusing such a breach of public trust, such a destruction of fundamental values for mercenary profits—and it's far from reassuring to find the Press and Enterprise lending its influence to such a sorry scheme.

H. H. BLISS.

Do We Want a San Jacinto Tramway?

Unlike the writer of a forceful letter in today's Open Forum, we find this a question on which well-intending men may differ.

The state parks, like the national parks, were created not only to preserve areas of unusual natural beauty but to give the people an opportunity to see and enjoy them. On the one hand we want to protect our wonderful natural inheritances; and on the other we want our people, the great highway traveling majority of them, to have the inspiration and refreshment which natural beauty offers. These interests are not easy to balance; the line between them is not easy to draw.

Those who take to the trails and even to the trailless wilderness get the most from nature; they are entitled to the exclusive use of some areas (although even their presence will in a strict sense disturb the balance of nature). But the far larger number who stick pretty close to the highways (some of them because of physical limitations) have some rights, too. Our bountiful heritage belongs to them also.

What does the tramway offer? A spectacular range of scenery (from desert sands to Alpine forests) and an inspirational view of our Colorado desert.

It would be the longest tramway in the world and its scenic rewards would be commensurate with its startling rise. Properly handled, it should interfere with the wilderness quality of only a small corner of the San Jacinto forest area.

Any detriment this involves seems to us to be outweighed by the values which the tramway offers.

APPENDIX F

AMENDED LANGUAGE OF ASSEMBLY BILL 3030

(Reprinted from California Legislature, A. B. 3030, 61st session (1955))

The original Section 2 of AB 3030 read,

The State Park Commission, acting through the Division of Beaches and Parks, shall provide for preservation and protection as a natural wilderness area of that portion of the State Park System formerly under the jurisdiction and control of the Mount San Jacinto Winter Park Authority, which portion of the State Park System shall be known as the Mount San Jacinto State Wilderness Area.

The amended language of AB 3030 read,

It is hereby declared that the policy of the State of California is to preserve, insofar as possible, certain areas within the State Park System as wilderness areas where this and future generations may enjoy the flora and fauna existing in such areas in a naturally uncultivated and uninhabited state. These areas would confer unlimited opportunities for cultural, spiritual, and recreational activities in nature, unchanged by man or by machine.

Unless the context otherwise specifically provides, the following definitions contained in this section shall govern the construction of this article:

"Wilderness area" means an areas uncultivated and set apart where natural geological, zoological, and botanical phenomena are undisturbed by the work of man or by machine.

Where the State Park Commission finds that an area in any state park is suitable to be preserved by and for the public as a wilderness area, the commission may declare that such area is to be preserved as a wilderness area.

Within a wilderness area there shall be no roads or other provisions for motorized or mechanical transportation, no commercial timber cutting, no occupancy under permits for hotels, stores, resorts, summer or winter homes, organization camps, hunting and fishing lodges or similar uses, no grazing of domestic or other livestock and no development of water storage other than as may be necessary for fire protection of the area.

Ingress and egress to a wilderness area shall be limited to travel on foot or on horseback.

The use of a wilderness area shall be limited to such activities as may be prescribed by the State Park Commission.

Any proposed change in the status of a wilderness area shall be given a public hearing after publication for four weeks in a newspaper of general circulation within the county in which such wilderness area is located. At any time prior to the time fixed for a hearing of the matter any person, association, or corporation may file with the State Park Commission, written objections to any such change.

There is in the State Park System, the Mount San Jacinto State Park which is owned by the State and in which is a wilderness area. The Division of Beaches and Parks shall provide for the preservation, protection, and conservation, as a wilderness area, of the high mountain country of the Mount San Jacinto State Park property comprising Sections 13 to 31, inclusive, of Township 4 South, Range 3 East, and the portions lying in Sections 6 and 7 of Range 3 East, Township 5 South and in Section 1 of Range 2 East, Township 5 South, San Bernardino Base and Meridian, in such way and in such manner as in its judgment may seem best and proper.

Except as is otherwise specified to the contrary in this article, all provisions of this chapter shall be applicable to wilderness areas.

APPENDIX G

EDITORIAL AND REBUTTALS

(Reprinted from the Riverside Enterprise, *April 20, 1955)*

For the Tramway

The county supervisors were, we feel, reflecting the views of the great majority of the people of Riverside county in the action they took Monday on the Mt. San Jacinto tramway question. They summarily rejected an appeal by certain conservation groups to endorse a bill which would repeal the act which authorizes the tramway's construction.

The question of whether the tramway should be built is one that has been debated so many times at every level of government concerned that everyone who is interested in it must, like four out of the five supervisors, have made up his mind by now. The tramway was authorized by a virtually unanimous vote of the legislature, and there has been no subsequent change in the factual situation which would call for any review.

Indeed the only change has been an increase in the need in Southern California for the type of recreational opportunity which the tramway would provide.

The conservation groups who oppose it so persistently have the best of motives, hut they misapply them. The thing about the tramway project that disturbs them is that, it will bring many more people to the wilderness area atop San Jacinto. And that's just the reason it should be built.

The experience of viewing the desert from the heights of this mountain is one that should not be restricted to the relatively small number who have the time and the physical endurance for a trail trip.

We are not and never have been in favor of opening up every area of natural beauty to everyone. We think that the highways and the tramways should be kept out of certain areas in order that they may be preserved in something like their, natural state and enjoyed in relative solitude. But the San Jacinto tramway offers too much in the way of recreational opportunity for too many people to be denied.

Actually the tramway is unlikely to bring any serious disturbance of the wilderness character of the area. The thousands of people who make the tram way ascent can he expected to spend their limited time enjoying the indescribably magnificent view, not in setting out on trail trips. This county has had little experience with tramways, but the country which has had the most (Switzerland) does not find that they mar or destroy natural values.

The trip from the floor of the Coachella Valley to the shoulder of Mt. San Jacinto will be one or the great tramway rides in the world. It will become one of the major scenic attractions of California. It will enable this county to offer the world a recreational opportunity that is new and worthwhile and different.

AGAINST THE TRAMWAY

Editor, the Press and Enterprise: I appreciate your concern in the editorial "For the Tramway" for the welfare of those who need the recreational opportunities available on Mount San Jacinto. Even more, I appreciate the following contradictory point that suggests that the thousands of people using the tram "can be expected to spend their limited time enjoying the indescribably magnificent view, not in setting out on trail trips,"

Well — what shall it be? A view? An eighth wonder of the world? Or a recreational wilderness area of inestimable value to our county and to the state?

This past summer the San Jacinto Primitive Area was used by youth groups from all six of our southern counties. State park records estimate 8000 man-days of use in the top country of the park. I have yet to find a Palm Springs horseman who looks with favor on construction of recreational facilities within the state park.

There is a right time and place for every right idea. In California's state parks there is not time and place ever for a supra-governmental authority.

According to the Mount San Jacinto Winter Park Authority Act of 1945, it has for the past 10 years been the "policy" of the people of this state to place jurisdiction of a state park (one set aside as a wilderness area with public funds) in the hands of a seven-man authority predominantly representative of Palm Springs commercial interests. The authority is given powers almost without limit to develop recreational facilities, clear ski slopes and pave parking areas and pathways, build structures, develop water and drainage facilities, and to lease concessions — all within the state park and on the top of the mountain.

Such provisions for use of a state park have never before been state policy. Such provisions for use of wilderness area forest and watershed lands are not the policy of the people of this State.

Nor is it policy of this state for a state park to be held liable for the debts and expenses of a state authority — though under the act the San Jacinto State Park would be liable to all uses provided for in the Act until the last bond was paid off. The probability of paying off bonds on a $15,000,000.00 to $30,000,000.00 project on top of our mountain is considered by conservative estimates to be highly improbable, to say the least.

It is our responsibility to see that our point of view is represented in the legal processes of our government. The laws that result are designed to govern us - and our lands.

April 27, in Sacramento, the Assembly Committee on Conservation will vote to pass or kill Assembly Bill 3030 — a bill presented to repeal the Mount San Jacinto Winter Park Authority Act, to provide for wilderness areas within oar State Park System, and to confirm Mount San Jacinto State Park's status as a wilderness area not to be utilized for commercial development of any kind.

This is an urgent moment. The people of Riverside County may, if they will, save their only forested high mountain from disuse and eventual destruction; they may save their own legislators from being party to shameful misapplication of "law."

Today, through letters and personal contacts, is the time to tell our elected representatives what we want our country politics to be -- whether we want tramways, concessions, and recreation resorts in our state parks; or watershed areas protected and state parks set aside for their value to all who wish to use them as natural areas, not as resorts.

ANA MARY ELLIOTT
Idyllwild

CONSERVATIONISTS' VIEW

Editor, the Press and Enterprise: Your editorial "For the Tramway" I feel does not fairly present the position taken by conservationists.

You say "the thing about the tramway project that disturbs them is that it will bring many more people to the wilderness atop San Jacinto."

Conservationists are not concerned about how many people are brought into the area so long as the natural aspects that make the area valuable are not destroyed, but we are alarmed when we think of turning thousands of people loose in a high fire area, few of whom are fire conscious, Fire fighting would be extremely difficult and expensive in this rugged country where there is but little available water. A large fire would destroy the very things on which the tramway is intended to capitalize.

Much is said about the wonderful view but the promoters do not seem to realize that since the days of smog and haze a clear view is seldom seen.

Conservationists object to having the very few available camp sites where water is available confiscated and commercialized by special interests thus robbing the 20,000 or more girl and boy scouts and other hiking campers who annually visit this area, of their rightful heritage.

We object to having the meager supply of water confiscated for human use thus driving out or destroying much wild animal life and blighting and destroying vegetation. The whole biological aspect of the area would be changed. Incidentally the campers would have to add to their already too heavy packs heavy supplies of water.

We object to commercializing this primitive area with hotels, cabins and eating houses as the primitive beauty of the area would soon be destroyed as has happened in many other parks.

We cannot have both the tramway and the primitive area. If the tramway goes in it will eventually destroy both the primitive area and itself.

A. K. WHIDDEN
Corona

APPENDIX H

REPORT OF THE SUBCOMMITTEE ON BEACHES ETC LAND CAPACITY SURVEYS FOR PARK AND RECREATIONAL AREAS

(California Legislature, Assembly, Interim Committee on Conservation, Planning, and Public Works, A State-Wide Park and Recreation Program. Report of the Subcommittee on Beaches and Parks, a Subcommittee of the Assembly Interim Committee on Conservation Planning and Public Works, Assembly Interim Committee reports, 1955-57, XII, No. 12 (March, 1957), pp. 61 – 62).

The Park Commission and the division have been under fire from special interest groups for restricted use of state park areas where the decisions on such control have not always been based upon sound conservation principles and best scientific methods to support these principles. Budgetary limitations in the past have, perhaps, been a factor preventing necessary surveys as basic to planning the development of state parks and recreation areas. One of the important guides for optimum use of such an area and consequently for development planning should be land use capacity surveys based on present knowledge regarding moisture, soils and cover. This subcommittee visited the San Jacinto Park and Wilderness Area as part of its interim studies. Its members traveled over the trails of this area on horseback during a full day trip and were impressed by the critical conditions of the trails and the cover even with the area's present limited use. These members are convinced that any more intensified use of the area should be based on its capacity determined by sound conservation principles. **The scientific determination of the best use of an area related to the conditions of the watershed and the preservation of the area itself appear appropriate criteria for deciding relative intensity of use and should be one of the tools available to the divisions of Recreation and Beaches and Parks in their planning process**. Thus, uses for grazing, hunting, timbering, should be justified or denied upon the bases of a plan of development wherein land, soil, and cover characteristics are the determining factors. These same types of conservation principles ought to determine the decisions regarding additional access roads and trails that would permit or prevent more intensified use.

The principle involved here is one of conservation. It is the belief of the subcommittee that this principle is more authoritative than some of the bases upon which current decisions are made controlling the use of park areas.

APPENDIX I

SOMEONE SHOULD AT LEAST SAY – "THANKS!"

(Editorial by Oliver B. Jaynes, reprinted from the Desert Sun, *December 27, 1956)*

The Tramway is dead--long live the Tramway!

Without even a memorial service—or a gathering of mourners—Mt. San Jacinto Aerial Tramway was laid quietly to rest last week. Scarred, bruised, and enfeebled by bad luck and pesky foes the "great idea" was given the coup de grace by the California State Park Board. Failure of the Park Board to renew a contract with the Tramway Authority to permit use of land in San Jacinto State Park for Tramway purposes was the death blow. Only formality now remaining is for the State Legislature to sign the death certificate.

Anyway, it must have been a very Merry Christmas for a rugged little band of nature lovers who have always wanted to preserve one of the world's most magnificent views for the enjoyment of their own eyes—and denied this inspiration to millions who could have seen it from the Tramway's top. Less hardy souls will have to be content to view the grandeur of this great mountain from afar since they can no longer hope to he lifted to its lofty heights in the comfort of a tram car.

Long, Sad Story

The story of the would-be tourist tramway (often incorrectly dubbed a "ski lift") would fill volumes. Since the day Francis Crocker first dreamed of making the thrilling view from one of the most precipitous mountains in North America available to millions, the idea was an inspiration to its advocates and a challenge to engineers. Planned to serve only the inspiration and delights of man, the projected giant was dogged all along the way because it had no more useful purpose.

Launched by the State Legislature (after two unsuccessful attempts), without a dollar to finance obviously needed preliminary work, the Tramway Authority had to depend for its support on the vision and generosity of those who believed in the idea. Perhaps more than a half million dollars for engineering studies and designs, surveys and many other preliminary costs was contributed by organizations and business firms. The world's most ambitious project of its kind was found to be feasible by the engineers. That it would be a financial success was also predicted by economists after a two-year study.

Handicapped by delays during two wars and constant harassment by the strong "conservationist" lobby, the Tramway Authority was plunged from one crisis into another. All the while, construction costs were mounting by the millions. Last known estimates passed the ten-million-dollar mark. From then on advocates could see the hand writing on the wall; the dream was doomed and its opponents were clamoring for the kill.

An All-Year Resort

There have always been a lot of people right here in Palm Springs who did not favor building the Tramway on the grounds that it would create a tourist-mob condition in a high class resort. Most support came from those who believed that this worldwide attraction would make Palm Springs a year-around resort through the thousands who would stop over in the summer months to take "the greatest trip on earth."

With the rapid growth of the area in the last few years, however, more and more people have come to believe that the Tramway would do more harm than good. Perhaps this is the reason there was little moaning at the bar when the Tramway dream put out to sea. Maybe it was because so many people had already given up. At any rate, the news did not seem to come at a great shock to the community.

Just Tram-View Village Remains

One wonders if there was ever before a community-sponsored project in the history of this country on which so many people spent so much time and money—with their dream unachieved. All there is to show for the long struggle are thousands of blueprints, legal documents and legislative measures collecting dust in files from coast to coast . . . and, of course . . . . Tram-View Village.

For all this time and effort and money someone should at least say "Thanks." The list of benefactors would be long and lustrous.

Perhaps the most disappointed man of all as he read the news last week in his Palo Alto home was former resident Edward Bacon, who offered to build the Tramway many years ago for $2,500.000—and has always believed that he could have done it.

APPENDIX J

THE TRAMWAY

(Editorial by Ernie Maxwell, reprinted from the Idyllwild Town Crier, *January 8, 1960)*

It's difficult to utter a simple "Yes" or "No" to questions and topics these days. Few of us possess even a fraction of the facts, and there seem to be so many variables.

Yet, we can state that we're opposed to the Mt. San Jacinto tramway project without too many qualifications. At the same time, we're ready to admit that the future picture can change to alter our present stand.

Basing our decision on 14 years on the hill, numerous snow treks into the Wild Area and studies of the proposal, we can't help but believe that the tramway is both unnecessary and impractical.

From experience we agree with testimony given at hearings that snow conditions surrounding the upper terminus are unsuited for winter sports. Skiers look upon the entire project as much too expensive for the small amount of sport that can be enjoyed anywhere near Long Valley.

The summer view from Mt. San Jacinto is no longer as spectacular as it may have been years ago. Today the haze and some smog reduce visibility during the warm months when no winds clear the desert area. Then, too, we have good views from Black Mt. and Santa Rosa, both accessible by car.

Therefore, without good snow and a view that isn't perfect year-round, justification of a multi-million dollar operation seems weak to us.

To put the tramway on a paying basis and prevent our backcountry from becoming the site of an abandoned mass of structures, calls for extensive commercialization at the top. This is permitted under provisions of the Winter Park Authority Act.

Concentrated human activity in any part of our Wild Area is regarded as detrimental. Vegetation grows slowly and the trampling by many feet can quickly change a scenic region into one of dust and pavement.

There is a limited water supply on top, as hikers and horsemen know. To obtain enough for a gigantic operation such as the tramway means tapping underground sources. This may affect local supplies.

Since 1945 when the tramway act was approved, both the Forest Service and state park have improved access trails in the Wild Area. From Humber Park it's now an easy walk. Therefore, the backcountry is accessible to almost anyone with a little effort.

Finally, the area was originally designated as a wilderness, and land was acquired with that understanding. The tramway destroys this classification and robs the state of its only high-mountain primitive type park.

We believe that the right thing to do is to hold Mt. San Jacinto State Park as it is for the next generation. If they wish to convert it into a luxurious resort that's their decision to make.

Appendix K

ATTITUDES HAVE CHANGED

(Editorial in The Desert Sun, *April 20, 1960)*

Were it not for the opposition of a small but somewhat Influential group of conservationists, the Mt. San Jacinto passenger tramway would likely have been built several years ago. While they were never able to block legislation that authorized the project, their harassment tactics caused numerous delays and made the work of the Tramway Authority a great deal more difficult.

This group of organized conservationists took the position that the scenic and primitive area which the tramway would make accessible to millions should be preserved for the few rugged individuals who could hike or pack in from Idyllwild. They opposed the project in spite of the fact that the area made accessible was limited in size and could not be commercialized. This protection was assured by a contract between the Tramway Authority and the State Park Board. The Desert Sun has always taken the position that thinking on the part of these organized conservationists was narrow and selfish.

This attitude that magnificent scenery and primitive areas should be reserved for the few, who wanted to enjoy solitary communication with nature, has undergone a change in the last few years. Students of land conservation for recreational purposes are coming to the belief that the tastes of the masses must be considered. They realize that frequent outings form an important phase of American life today; that it is vital to the well-being of the average citizen. . . . .

. . . . social conservation must include not only such activities as fishing, hunting, boating, swimming, golf, and hiking but also outings not in the realm of sport. Sightseeing, for example. Probably as many people go just for a day's outing in the car as participate in all the sports combined. Our mountain and desert scenery lures countless thousands each week from the cities and towns into the wide open spaces.

The Mt. Jacinto Tramway would make possible an outing for those who do not—or cannot—go in for swimming, fishing, hunting, boating and the like. It would open up a good skiing area but it is planned as a sightseeing attraction and not as a ski lift, as some people thought. The view from the summit would be one of the most spectacular in California. It would be financed by revenue bonds and revert to the State of California when the bonds were paid off.

Whether or not the tramway will ever be built is anybody's guess. Some of the project's original supporters have lost interest; a few residents never did favor it. No one can deny that it would be one of the state's greatest outdoor attractions.

Meanwhile, the Division of Beaches and Parks has drawn up an agreement under which the Tramway Authority could resume efforts to sell the bonds and start construction. The contract is now under study by the Department of Natural Resources and the Department of Finance of the state government. It will be a few months before these agencies report. So the 15-year battle for the Mt. San Jacinto Tramway is still being waged.

If they have not wrecked it beyond repair, the band of narrow-minded conservationists will discover it more difficult now to find people in sympathy with their arguments against the long sought project. They will find that sentiment has changed over the years—like the engineering advancement that would make it possible to build the tramway in one span instead of two as originally planned.

Bibliography/References Cited

America's First Aerial Tramway. Cannon Mountain Aerial Passenger Tramway, Franconia Notch, New Hampshire: 1938.

Banning *Record*, various dates as cited in text.

"Cannon History." http://cannonmt.com/cannon-history.html, accessed April 2, 2016.

Clark, Nathan C. "Nathan C. Clark - Sierra Club Leader, Outdoorsman, & Engineer." Interview by Richard Searle. Sierra Club History Committee: 1977.

Cole, David, and Thomas Carlson. *Numerical Visitor Capacity: A Guide to its Use in Wilderness.* U. S. Department of Agriculture, Forest Service, Rocky Mountain Research Station, Fort Collins, Colorado: 2010.

Coverdale and Colpitts. "Report on Economic Feasibility – Proposed Mount San Jacinto Aerial Tramway Project, Palm Springs, California." New York, New York: May 4, 1956.

Davis, Richard Carter. "Wilderness, Politics, and Bureaucracy: Federal and State Policies in the Administration of San Jacinto Mountain, Southern California, 1920 - 1968." Ph.D. Dissertation, University of California, Riverside, Riverside, California: August, 1973.

Dawson, Glenn. "Ski Touring and Ski Mountaineering." Trails Magazine (The Mountain League of Southern California), Vol. 5, No. 4, Autumn, 1938, pp 8-10.

The Desert Sun, various dates as cited in text.

Everson, Hazel. "Skiing Has Come to Stay." Trails Magazine (The Mountain League of Southern California), Vol. 4, No. 4, Autumn, 1937, pp 8-11, 19.

Fleming, Guy. "Shall We Cherish and Maintain the San Jacinto Wild Area?" Sierra Club Bulletin, October, 1949, pp. 4-10.

Fleming, Guy. "The Mount San Jacinto Tramway Scheme." National Parks Magazine, April-June 1949: pp. 21-25.

Gilligan, James Pershing. "The Development of Policy and Administration of Forest Service Primitive and Wilderness Areas in the Western United States." Ph.D. Dissertation, University of Michigan, Ann Arbor, Michigan: 1953.

Godfrey, Anthony. *The Ever-Changing View – A History of the National Forests in California, 1891-1987.* USDA Forest Service, July 2005.

Hall, Harvey Monroe. "A Botanical Survey of San Jacinto Mountain." University of California Publications in Botany, Vol. 1, No. 1, University Press, Berkeley, California: 1902.

Hauk, A. Andrew (Vice-president of the Far West Ski Association), and Lute Holley (Chairman, Area Development Committee of the Far West Ski Association). Editorial in *The Skier*, March 1, 1949, p. 2.

Hemet *News*, various dates as cited in text.

Hendee, John C., George H. Stankey, and Robert C. Lucas. *Wilderness Management.* U. S. Department of Agriculture Forest Service Miscellaneous Publication Number 1365; October, 1978.

James, Harry. "The Mt. San Jacinto Winter Park Summer Resort Scheme." The Living Wilderness (publication of The Wilderness Society) No. 31, pp. 4-16: Winter, 1949-1950.

Jennings, Bill. "Memorial to Harry Clebourne James." Journal of California and Great Basin Anthropology, Vol. 1, Issue 1: 1979. Retrieved from https://escholarship.org/uc/item/4060c2ck February 13, 2021.

Kieley, Kitty (granddaughter of O. Earl Coffman). Personal communication with the author, as cited in text.

Landells, James. *We Can Do It: The Construction of the Palm Springs Aerial Tramway.* Arrow Printing, Palm Springs, California: 2012.

Lech, Steve. *Along the Old Roads - A History of the Portion of Southern California That Became Riverside County, 1772-1893.* Published by the author, Riverside, California: 2004.

Lech, Steve. *For Tourism and a Good Night's Sleep – J. Win Wilson, Wilson Howell, and the Beginnings of the Pines-to-Palms Highway*. Published by the author, Riverside, California: 2012.

Lech, Steve. *More Than a Place to Pitch a Tent – The Stories Behind Riverside County's Regional Parks*. Published by the author, Riverside, California: 2011.

Leopold, Aldo. "The Wilderness and Its Place in Forest Recreational Policy." Journal of Forestry, Volume 19, Issue 7, November 1921, Pages 718–721. Accessed at https://doi.org/10.1093/jof/19.7.718 on February 8, 2021.

Los Angeles *Times*, various dates as cited in text.

Maxwell, Ernie. "Mount San Jacinto – Tramway or Wilderness?" Pacific Discovery Magazine, Vol. VIII, No. I, pp. 21 - 23: January-February, 1955.

Miller, Rex. "Where Summer and Winter Join Hands." The Christian Science Monitor, March 9, 1940.

Modjeski and Masters (consulting engineers). "Report on the Proposed Passenger Tramway up Mt. San Jacinto at Palm Springs, California." April, 1940.

Momyer, Joseph. "San Jacinto: The Promoter's Nightmare." Sierra Club Bulletin, Vol. XL, pp. 17 – 18: January, 1955.

New England Ski History, Cannon Mountain, Franconia New Hampshire. http://www.newenglandskihistory.com/NewHampshire/cannonmtn.php, accessed March 26, 2016.

Official Statement of Mount San Jacinto Winter Park Authority (California) Relating to $7,700,000 5½% Mount San Jacinto Winter Park Authority Revenue Bonds, Series A, Palm Springs, California, June 14, 1961.

Palm Springs *Limelight*, various dates as cited in text.

Riverside *Enterprise*, various dates as cited in text.

Riverside *Press*, various dates as cited in text.

Robinson, John W. and Bruce D. Risher. *The San Jacintos*. Big Santa Anita Historical Society, Arcadia, California: 1993.

Samuelson, Val. "To the Haunts of Tahquitz." Pacific Discovery Magazine, Vol. VIII, No. I, pp. 15 – 20: January-February, 1955.

Smith, DeBoyd Leon. *A Study of the Human Use of the Mount San Jacinto Wild Area in the San Jacinto Mountain Range and the Surrounding San Bernardino National Forest Area*. Unpublished paper presented in Natural Science 298, Long Beach State College: 1957.

State of California, "Agreement" (AG-7/18/1960), August 4, 1960.

Sumner, E. Lowell. *Special Report on a Wildlife Study in the High Sierra in Sequoia and Yosemite National Parks and Adjacent Territory*. U.S. National Park Service Records, National Archives, Washington, DC: 1936.

"Trailfinders History." Website of the James San Jacinto Mountains Reserve, Natural Reserve System. https://james.ucnrs.org/trail-finders-history/. Accessed February 13, 2021.

Wicken, Ingrid P. *Pray for Snow: This History of Skiing in Southern California*. Vasa Press, Norco, California: 2002.

Wicken, Ingrid P. Personal communication with the author, October 12, 2021.

TRAMBI

Constructing Tower 1 from the ground (Palm Springs Aerial Tramway photo).

About the Author

Steve Lech is a native Riversider who has been interested in the history of Riverside County for more than 40 years, and has written or co-written more than a dozen books and over 300 articles on various aspects of Riverside County's history. In addition to writing and researching articles and books, he serves as co-editor of the Riverside County Chronicles (the Riverside County Heritage Association's journal of local history), is on the editorial board of the Journal of the Riverside Historical Society, and has also been the editor of the Branding Iron, the newsletter of the Los Angeles Corral of the Westerners. He is president of the Riverside Historical Society and the Riverside County Heritage Association and maintains memberships in some two dozen other local historical societies throughout Riverside County and Southern California. Steve is a long-time member of the Riverside County Historical Commission, and has been on the City of Riverside's Cultural Heritage Board and Historic Preservation Fund Committee. He has been a docent with the Mission Inn Foundation in Riverside since September, 1988, has been the Director of Docent Training for the MIF since 2019, and is an active member of the MIF History Research Committee which seeks to document the many stories that surround Riverside's historic hotel. Steve retired from the County of Riverside in 2014 so he could continue to research many aspects of Riverside County's varied history.